WILD AT HEART

FIELD GUIDE

A MAP TO RECOVER YOUR MASCULINE HEART

REVISED EDITION

JOHN ELDREDGE

NELSON
BOOKS

An Imprint of Thomas Nelson

OTHER BOOKS BY JOHN ELDREDGE

All Things New

Beautiful Outlaw

Captivating (with Stasi Eldredge)

Epic

Fathered by God

Free to Live

Get Your Life Back

The Journey of Desire

Killing Lions (with Samuel Eldredge)

Knowing the Heart of God

Love and War (with Stasi Eldredge)

Moving Mountains

The Sacred Romance (with Brent Curtis)

Waking the Dead

Walking with God

Wild at Heart

Wild at Heart Field Guide (Revised Edition)
© 2002, 2021 by John Eldredge

The personal identities of the persons quoted in the *Wild at Heart Field Guide* have been disguised in order to protect their privacy. Published in Nashville, Tennessee, by Nelson Books. Nelson Books is a registered trademark of HarperCollins Christian Publishing, Inc.

Published in association with Yates & Yates, LLP, Literary Agents, Orange, California.

Unless otherwise noted, Scripture quotations are from the Holy Bible: New International Version®. Copyright © 1973, 1978, 1984, 2011 by International Bible Society. Used by permission of Zondervan Publishing House. All rights reserved.

Scripture quotations marked NIV 84 are taken from the Holy Bible: New International Version®. Copyright © 1973, 1978, 1984 by International Bible Society. Used by permission of Zondervan Publishing House. All rights reserved.

Scripture quotations marked NKJV are taken from The New King James Version®. Copyright © 1982 by Thomas Nelson. Used by permission. All rights reserved.

Scripture quotations marked THE MESSAGE are taken from *The Message: The New Testament in Contemporary English*. Copyright © 1993 by Eugene H. Peterson.

Scripture quotations marked NLT are taken from the Holy Bible, New Living Translation, copyright © 1996. Used by permission of Tyndale House Publishers, Inc., Wheaton, Illinois 60189. All rights reserved.

Scripture quotations marked NASB are taken from the New American Standard Bible®, © Copyright The Lockman Foundation 1960, 1962, 1963, 1968, 1971, 1972, 1973, 1975, 1977, 1995. Used by permission (www.Lockman.org).

ISBN 978-0-310-13564-7 (softcover)
ISBN 978-0-310-13565-4 (ebook)

First Printing January 2021

CONTENTS

INTRODUCTION

It was dark by the time we clipped in. Pitch-dark, as in, there was no moon. Our climbing adventure had changed without notice into something else—something more like survival. That wasn't our intent, it's just that we'd started our climb a little later in the day than we wanted, and then ran into some snags as my partner and I worked our way up the face of Saddle Rock, somewhere in the deserts of Southern California. We'd made it about halfway when the sun went down and we found ourselves faced with a choice to try to finish the ascent in the dark, or rappel down. Discretion seemed the better part of valor at this point, so we chose to rappel. My partner, who was a much better climber than I, went first.

He disappeared over the edge, leaning backward and stepping off into the black. I waited in silence for him to make the ledge below. After what seemed like a half hour or more (but was probably only minutes), I heard a faint holler for me to follow. As I looped the rope through my ATC, a voice inside was yelling at me: *What do you think you're doing? Why do you do this to yourself? You're always getting yourself into messes like this.* You see, I'd climbed a bit before this night, but I'd never rappelled in my life and my first lesson was about to take place in utter darkness down a foreign face of rock to a ledge about a foot wide, which we guessed was sitting about 130 feet off the valley floor below. *Well,* I thought, *I can't exactly stay here. The only way out of this mess is over that edge.* With that, I leaned back into the void.

OVER THE EDGE

You are standing on the brink of what could be the greatest adventure you've ever known . . . and your fiercest battle.

When it comes to the story of your life, and how it will be told ages hence around the campfires of the kingdom, the central chapter will be your masculine journey. That journey is the essential quest of your life, whereby you recover your true heart, discover your real name, and find your place in the battle. Everything else flows from there.

It's hard. It's scary. And it's worth it.

There is a life that few men know . . . a life so rich and free, so dangerous and yet so exhilarating in its impact that if you knew now what you *could* have, you would sell everything to find it. But you have a sense of it even now, from the echoes in your heart, the hints in your deepest desires, the Voice that has been calling you for a long time, and that's why you're holding this field guide.

I'm proud of you. It took guts to get this far, and you are about to enter an elite company of men. This will be a major turning point in your life—maybe *the* turning point. Behind is the life you've led; ahead lies your destiny. Before you clip in and step off, let me say a few things.

I offer this field guide as a map for your masculine journey, the rope you'll use to go over the edge. It's going to look a little dark at times, and my hunch is there'll be moments when you'll feel something of the fear and the *What am I doing?* feeling I was having halfway up the rock that night. That's normal, and healthy, and part of the journey. Having said that, let me try to offer some thoughts on how to use this guide.

DON'T RUSH

You'll notice we didn't call this a "workbook" or a "curriculum." You're embarking on a journey, not doing your homework. Approach it like that. Take your time; find your stride. If certain questions don't seem to help, skip 'em for those that do. You're not memorizing answers; you're reclaiming your *heart*. Don't force this work to fit into a neat, classroom experience.

UNDERSTAND IT'S A BATTLE

You're going to experience a lot of different emotions and hear a lot of thoughts as you go through this. Things like, *I don't have time to get to this right now* or *This may be for other guys, but not for me* or *I'm just a poser*. About 99 percent of that is from the Enemy. He fears what will happen if you take this journey. Fight those thoughts and emotions and press on.

ON THE MOVIES I RECOMMEND

A Christian author is recommending R-rated movies??? How can that be?

First, I want to say that when I recommend a movie, I am not endorsing its every scene. I do not enjoy violence myself, and I will often look away during the bloody scenes of *Gladiator* or *Braveheart*. And I always guard my heart by not indulging in scenes I find sexually inappropriate. However, I want to point out that the Bible has some pretty strong scenes in it as well—rape, dismemberment, murder, bloody battle, and more.

At the start of each chapter I recommend films that address crucial themes for men. As one man just wrote to me,

> Now I understand why movies like *A Perfect World* and *Good Will Hunting* (and *The Godfather* and *Scent of a Woman*) have resonated with me. I used to think that I was nothing more than a worldly heathen for being touched by those "ungodly" movies. I see now that the central theme of each one of those films is something I myself have longed for—the impartation of masculinity from fathers (or father figures) to their sons. And that it's not just okay to like them, but essential to my healing to study and apply their messages.

Watch each one if at all possible, before you do the work on that chapter. It will really open things up for you.

THE "FIELD NOTES"

I asked my publisher to try to provide plenty of space in the journal for capturing thoughts, grabbing ideas, writing down your prayers and reactions as you go along. That's what the Field Notes pages are for. Use them to note more questions or ideas that grab you.

SHARING THE JOURNEY

Many of you will take this journey alone . . . for now. That, too, is part of your quest—going into the wilderness with God alone.

But eventually, every one of us needs a band of brothers. Not accountability partners, but guys we can take a journey with, go to battle alongside. This field guide could be a powerful way to bring that band together or deepen the journey of your existing band. Let me offer a few thoughts, then, for men doing this together . . .

Swear to absolute confidentiality. Nothing shared in the group gets repeated outside the group, unless permission is given. This is so important I'd make it an act of automatic expulsion for the man who violates the covenant.

Do not rush through simply to meet some sort of deadline. Don't force the journey into a twelve-week format. There are certain chapters that will take you several meetings to work through, so that every man can share in the interaction.

Everybody should read the book first, to give you the big picture and put all men on the same page.

I'd recommend sharing your stories as you go along. Only when we understand another man's story can we help him in his journey, for then we have a better view of what he's endured, what the Enemy has been up to, and how God is working in his life.

Be very slow—very—to offer advice. This is in many ways a journey of self-discovery. Yet there are certain men who feel the need to "teach" in a group setting. Tell 'em to knock it off.

Try not to do this in an overly "religious" setting. Make it real. Meet in a home. You could watch the movies, or at least a key scene from them that way, as part of your meeting. I know some guys who are doing it at a laid-back coffee house and others who meet in a pub. The point is, you don't want this to feel "religious." That'll kill it quickly.

Watch the movies together. If you can't pull it off, at least watch a scene from each chapter's movie together, to help pull you into the discussion.

Adventure together. Do something that gets past the awkwardness of just meeting each week to "share." Shoot some hoops. Go fishing. Hit the batting cages. I took a group of guys backpacking this summer, and we sort of went through the key ideas a day at a time. I'd pose a key question in the morning like, "What did your dad tell you about yourself as a man?" or "What has the woman meant to you over the years?" We'd think about it all day and then talk it over around the campfire in the evening.

See it through to the end.

WHAT ABOUT YOUR WOMAN?

This journey is a masculine journey; you'll take it alone, or with a few other men. I wouldn't take your first pass through this guide with your woman. But at some point, you'll want her to read *Wild at Heart*, too. Every woman I've spoken to has loved it. Besides, this is so revolutionary, she needs to have a clue what you're up to and why you're suddenly acting the way you are. I'll offer some thoughts for how to bring her in as you go along in the journey itself.

STEPPING OFF

Once again, let me say it with all honesty: I'm proud of you. We need you in this revolution. It's going to get a little messy and bloody, and that's just the way it goes. But remember,

> It is not the critic who counts, not the man who points out how the strong man stumbles, or where the doer of deeds could have done them better. The credit belongs to the man in the arena, whose face is marred by dust and sweat and blood; who strives valiantly . . . who knows the great enthusiasms, the great devotions; who spends himself in a worthy cause; who at the best knows in the end the triumph of high achievement, and who at the worst, if he fails, at least fails while daring greatly, so that his place shall never be with those cold and timid souls who have never known neither victory nor defeat.
>
> Teddy Roosevelt

If that is the man you want to be, then press on.

There are many in the great cloud of witnesses cheering for you. I am one of them.

John

CHAPTER 1

WILD AT HEART

The spiritual life cannot be made suburban.
It is always frontier, and we who live in it must accept
and even rejoice that it remains untamed.

HOWARD MACEY

BEFORE SETTING OUT

I want to *strongly* urge you to do three things before you start working through this chapter.

First, it would be a really good idea to go and watch one of your favorite movies again—one of the epics, not a nonsense comedy. Sure—a lot of us had a good laugh over *Caddyshack*, but your work here requires something deeper, at the level of the soul. I mention some of the old classics like *The Bridge on the River Kwai*, *Shane*, and *High Noon*. Or you might choose an epic such as *Rocky*, *Saving Private Ryan*, or *Gladiator*. More recently I found the movie *Fury* to be profound, as well as *Man of Steel*. Better still, get together with a few buddies and watch it together. What does it stir in your masculine heart?

Second, you need to Get Out! Get outside. It may not seem totally clear at this point why, but it will become clearer as you go on. Get out, away from the cell phone and the TV and the chatter of your world. Get to the mountains, or the sea, to a stream or cornfield, or even just to the park, and spend some time there. That would be a great place to reread chapter 1 in the book, and if you have the

time, to take some of the expedition below. Don't make excuses, don't dismiss this . . . do it. Take a whole weekend away and do several chapters!

Third, reread chapter 1 in the book, if it's been more than a week since you read it. You'd be surprised how much gets lost after a week.

GUT REACTION

You've read the first chapter in *Wild at Heart*—now give me a gut reaction. What struck you? What stirred you, got your blood going? Did anything grab you, frustrate you, make you mad? What questions did it raise? Was there a major "aha!," a revelation of some kind? What did it make you want to *do*? Don't bother to edit your thoughts here. And don't try to make them sound "spiritual" or "manly" or whatever. Just be honest.

GETTING YOUR BEARINGS

The Goal
This chapter isn't about fixing or solving anything . . . including you. Instead, I merely want to *awaken* something. I want to arouse that masculine heart that so often slumbers down under the surface of your life. I want to give it permission to come out of hiding and give you some clarity and, more importantly, *validation*. Your journey starts there.

Trail Markers

- Men and women bear the image of God either *as men* or *as women*.
- There is, therefore, something deep and true and universal to the masculine heart.
- And it's been lost—or better, driven into hiding.
- To get your masculine heart back, you cannot begin with more duty and obligation. You must begin with your deepest desires. *What makes you come alive?*
- Somewhere down in your heart are three core desires: a battle to fight, an adventure to live, and a beauty to love.

SETTING OUT

Did the chapter validate anything about you? Did it give you a kind of permission? In what way?

I hope you did watch one of your favorite films, and if you did, what did it stir in you this time around?

Here's the deal: God meant something when he meant man—when he meant *you*—and if we are to ever find ourselves we must find that. What has he set in the masculine heart? More importantly, what has God set in *your* masculine heart? It's an elusive prey you're after, to be sure. So start with something readily at hand—movies. I believe that the movies you love are a clue to your heart, to what makes you come alive. So let's start there. Write down a handful of movies that have stirred your heart over the years.

And from those stories what roles, what heroes would you love to play? Who would you love to be in those movies? (I'd love to be Scott Glen in *Silverado*, Maximus in *Gladiator*, or William Wallace in *Braveheart*.)

FIELD NOTES

A BREAK IN THE CLOUDS

Is this exercise hard for you? Do you find it tough to come up with much? I'm not surprised—as I said, our heart has been driven into remote regions of the soul. It takes time to track it down.

Another way of getting below the surface, to the real desires of our hearts, is to look at what we do with our free time. Set a man completely free, and simply watch what he does. You'll learn a lot. Let's say you have three months of vacation coming up, a sabbatical all to yourself, and plenty of cash to bankroll it. Where would you go? What would you do? What's your "dream trip"?

Looking back now at the movies you love, the roles you'd want to play, and your three-month daydream, what does it tell you about your own heart? What are you made for?

A BATTLE TO FIGHT

Remember back into your boyhood for a moment. Did you play games involving battles? Cowboys and Indians, perhaps, or maybe cops and robbers? What were they? What do your sons or grandsons love to play?

I talked about my favorite Christmas present ever—two pearl-handled six-shooters, black leather holsters, red cowboy shirt with two wild mustangs embroidered on either breast, shiny black boots, red bandanna, and straw hat. I didn't take it off for weeks because it was not a "costume" at all; it was an *identity*. Who did you love to be as a boy? Did you have a favorite outfit you wore?

What was the "necessary equipment"—tangerine grenades, trash-can-lid shields, a Spider Man outfit, a light saber?

And who were your boyhood heroes? An army man, an athlete, or maybe a cowboy, a superhero like Batman or Superman? Did they have a great battle to fight?

Look back now at your favorite movies you jotted down. What is the hero's great battle? Which of those battles would *you* love to fight, if you were he?

Now, this longing may have submerged from years of neglect, and a man may not feel that he is up to the battles he knows await him. Or it may have taken a very dark turn, as it has with inner-city gangs. But the desire is there. Every man wants to play the hero. I find that many men have long buried their desire to be a hero. But isn't there something in you that wants to be applauded, cheered for what you've done? Do you like losing, for example—or being dismissed? What debate would you love to win, what deal would you love to land, what "big fish" would you love to catch, what hill would you love to take?

WARNING!

I know a number of good men who don't really resonate with actual battle involving bloodshed. So please understand that when I refer to battle, it may not be guns and swords, but a battle for a principle or a great cause. I think of *Chariots of Fire*, where Eric Liddle stands alone for his faith. Or *Schindler's List*, where Schindler "fights" the Nazis with cunning as he rescues Jews by employing them.

Every man needs to know that he is powerful. Women didn't make *Braveheart* one of the best-selling films of the decade. *Flying Tigers, The Bridge on the River Kwai, The Magnificent Seven, Shane, High Noon, Saving Private Ryan, Top Gun,* the *Die Hard* films, *Gladiator*—the movies a man loves reveal what his heart longs for, what is set inside him from the day of his birth. Like it or not, there is something fierce in the heart of every man.

What happens in you when you watch one of those powerful stories, when at the end of *Braveheart* the "starving and outnumbered" Scots rush the fields at Bannockburn and win their freedom, or when Maximus goes hand-to-hand with Commodus at the end of *Gladiator*? Is there anything in a great battle scene that stirs your heart? Can you sense something fierce down in there?

Sometimes our aggression has no place to play itself out, except maybe in sports or how we drive. Do you ever want to just slam-dunk something, knock something into kingdom come? Do you like it when people pass you on the highway, or beat you to a parking spot? Where does your *aggressive* side surface?

Closer to home, what if a terrorist broke into your house tonight and threatened the lives of your wife and children—would you simply let it happen? If you were armed, would you use your weapon? Do you sense something fierce in your own heart now?

Have you ever been told that such fierceness is a *good* thing?

ADVENTURE

I'm convinced that adventure, with all its requisite danger and wildness, is a deeply spiritual longing written into the soul of man. Does that surprise you, hearing that adventure is a *spiritual* longing given to us by God?

Return again to boyhood. When I was seven, I tried to dig a hole to China from our backyard with my friend Danny Wilson. We gave up at about eight feet, but it made a great fort. Hannibal crosses his famous Alps, and there comes a day in a boy's life when he first crosses the street and enters the company of the great explorers. Scott and Amundsen race for the South Pole, Peary and Cook vie for the North, and one summer, many years ago, when I gave my boys some loose change and permission to ride their bikes down to the store to buy a soda, you'd have thought I'd given them a charter to go find the equator.

What were some of the "great adventures" you had—or dreamed of or read about—as a boy?

I remember as a boy, loving to walk trails in the woods, always wondering what was around the corner and what I would find. I didn't get to do it much, but the times I did left an indelible impression in my mind. Even then my heavenly Father was stirring me for my own trail, the one he made just for me . . .

My great-grandfather was a full-blooded Irishman born in Ireland. I've never been there, and I would love to make a pilgrimage, to travel home for the first time and ceremonialize the Ultimate Adventure God has for my life!

SKIP

This isn't just about boyhood either. I told you about that judge in his sixties, a real Southern gentleman with a pin-striped suit and an elegant manner whom I met at a conference, and how he told me the story of the storm off Bermuda. "It came up out of nowhere. Twenty-foot swells in a thirty-foot homemade boat. I thought we were all going to die." A pause for dramatic effect, and then he confessed, "It was the best time of my life." Describe an adventure you've had in more recent years, a time when you really came alive. What happened? What did it require of you?

ON WILDERNESS

Eve was created within the lush beauty of Eden's garden. But Adam, if you'll remember, was created *outside* the garden, in the wilderness. In the record of our beginnings, the second chapter of Genesis makes it clear: Man was born in the outback, from the untamed part of creation. Only afterward was he brought to Eden. And ever since then boys have never been at home indoors, and men have an insatiable longing to explore. We long to return to the outdoors; it's when most men come alive. As John Muir said, when a man comes to the mountains, he comes home.

Have you ever spent time in the outdoors? Did you enjoy it?

On page 4 of the book, I mention a North Face ad that says, "I am not alive in an office. I am not alive in a taxicab. I am not alive on a sidewalk." Where *do* you most come alive?

Look at the heroes of the biblical text: Moses does not encounter the living God at the mall. He finds him (or is found by him) somewhere out in the deserts of Sinai, a long way from the comforts of Egypt. The same is true of Jacob, who has his wrestling match with God not on the living room sofa but in a wadi somewhere east of the Jabbok, in Mesopotamia. Where did the great prophet Elijah go to recover his spiritual strength? To the wild. As did John the Baptist, and his cousin, Jesus, who was *led by the Spirit* into the wilderness.

The early Celtic Christians called the Holy Spirit the Wild Goose. They knew that following him meant accepting a great adventure. Has the Spirit ever led you

FIELD NOTES

A BREAK IN THE CLOUDS

I am high above the timberline
Where the sky and mountains meet
Up where the air is very thin
Somehow it's easier to breathe
Like the wind in the canyon echoing
The spirit is calling me, whispering
Out here
In the wild and the wonder
Where the lightning and the thunder
Serve a great awakening
Out here
Where the One who did the making
Is still in me creating
A place where I am free
I can hear
I can breathe
I believe
Out here

"OUT HERE," BY GEOFF MOORE
AND JEFF SILVEY;
1999; from the Geoff Moore CD

into the wilderness—a calling, or a haunting to just "get away from it all," get out into the wild? If he did so now, would you go?

The fact is, adventure *requires* something of us, puts us to the test. Though we may fear the test, at the same time we yearn to be tested, to discover that we have what it takes . . . If a man has lost this desire, says he doesn't want it, that's only because he doesn't know if he has what it takes or believes that he will fail the test. And so he decides it's better not to try. But you can't escape it—there is something wild in the heart of every man. Have you ever seen, in your desires or even in your fantasies, something "wild" (risky, adventurous, undomesticated) in your own heart?

And have you understood that wildness to be a good thing? Would you like there to be a wildness about you?

A BEAUTY TO LOVE

I didn't need to tell you that there's nothing so inspiring as a beautiful woman, now, did I? She'll make you want to charge the castle, slay the giant, leap across the parapets. We all know this—a man wants to be the hero to the Beauty. It's not enough to be a hero; it's that he is a hero *to someone* in particular, to the woman he loves. Remember the first time you fell in love—what was her name? Where did you meet? What was it about her that turned your head, captured your heart?

And think back again to the movie roles you'd love to play—who are the damsels you'd love to fight for?

And, recalling the daydream about three months of free time and anything you could do, would the months really be everything you desire if there were only adventure but never a beautiful woman as part of that adventure?

Now, maybe that passion hasn't always taken a good direction, and maybe you haven't been able to live it out for other reasons, but setting all other issues aside for the moment—can you see that there is something passionate in your heart when it comes to the Beauty? What stirs inside you when you look upon the daughters of Eve?

WARNING!

I am not encouraging lust. To see a beautiful woman and admire her beauty is not lust at all. However, to undress her in your mind and crave her for your own sexual pleasure is another matter. Many good men live with unnecessary guilt because they, like any red-blooded male, are struck by a woman's beauty. A captivating woman is one of the most striking aspects of God's creation; she was meant to be. To say she must not have an effect on us is like saying we should not be moved by a beautiful symphony unless we wrote it, or that we mustn't be awestruck by a sunset because it's not our sunset.

And have you sensed that, at its core, your passion to love the Beauty is a good thing, part of your destiny?

ON EVE

What was your reaction to read that the three desires of a woman's heart are to be fought for, to be invited up into a great adventure, and to unveil her beauty? Can you see that now in what she loves and longs for?

Would you be willing to ask the Eve in your life about her desires? Ask her about her favorite movies and why she loves them. Ask her what she'd do with three months of vacation, what her "dream trip" would be.

SOMETHING'S BEEN LOST

The way a man's life unfolds nowadays tends to drive his heart into remote regions of the soul. Endless hours at a computer screen; selling shoes at the mall; meetings, memos, phone calls. The business world—where the majority of American men live and die—requires a man to be efficient and punctual. Corporate policies and procedures are designed with one aim: to harness a man to the plow and make him produce.

How much room for your masculine soul—for adventure and battle and beauty—is there in your typical week?

The masculine heart needs a place where nothing is prefabricated, modular, nonfat, zip-locked, franchised, online, microwavable. Where there are no deadlines, cell phones, or committee meetings. Where there is room for the soul. Where, finally, the geography around us corresponds to the geography of our heart. How would you describe the "geography" of your daily world—does it fit the terrain of your deep heart?

The reason most messages for men ultimately fail is simply because they ignore what is most deep and true to a man's heart and simply try to produce external changes through various forms of pressure. "This is the man you *ought* to be. This is what a good husband/father/Christian/churchgoer *ought* to do." Fill in the blank from there. He is responsible, sensitive, disciplined, faithful, diligent, dutiful, etc.

Think about your life, your world. What is being asked of you? What do you feel the *pressure* to be . . .

At home?

DISPATCH

I have been hearing a voice all my life. Not different voices, but the same voice. As a boy, the voice shouted at me from the pages of Louis L'Amour's books. I heard the voice say that one day I would be the hero that I was reading about. I would be strong and courageous, faithful and true. I would always come through in the clutch for those I loved. My heart would one day find my heroine, and together we would build a life and a family. I knew there would be tough times and defeats. We would sometimes suffer wounds and even lose battles and fights, but would triumph in the end. The voice spoke to me through movies . . . *Rocky, Uncommon Valor, The Man from Snowy River.*

Why can't I hear the voice all the time? Whose voice is it? How do I respond? Who's calling?

FRED

At work?

At church?

At a recent church retreat I was talking with a guy in his fifties, listening really, about his own journey as a man. "I've pretty much tried for the last twenty years to be a good man as the church defines it." Intrigued, I asked him to say what he thought that was. He paused for a long moment. "Dutiful," he said. "And separated from his heart."

Would you agree with this man's assessment of what the church defines a good man to be? What would you say is the commonly held view in your church when it comes to a good Christian man? (Think of the guys held up as models in your church.)

And yet, because of the way in which we bear the image of God, because Adam was drawn not from Eden but from the outback of creation, "The core of a man's heart is undomesticated, *and that is good*." That's why Cole Porter sang, "Don't fence me in." Do you have any place in your world where you are actually encouraged to be undomesticated? Or is the leash on you pretty short? How "fenced in" are you?

FIELD NOTES

DISPATCH

I am twenty-nine, with a wife, five-year-old son, mortgage, car payment, and second child due in December. And God, I'm bored! My whole life I've wanted more . . . but the cares of this world have always choked out the seeds of desire.

MARVIN

SO WHERE DOES THAT LEAVE YOU?

You see, there is the life we were *meant for* and the man we were *created to be* . . . and then there is the life we *have* and the man we *find ourselves* to be. They are often worlds apart.

What is your great battle? Is it merely on the level of making more money, or getting the kids to behave, reducing the hassles of life?

Where is your great adventure? What risky venture have you been swept up into? Is there anything larger in your life than sports, or stocks, or watching the adventures of others on TV?

And who is the Beauty you are fighting for? Is there a woman in your life who stirs you to leap from the falls to win her?

AN INVITATION—PERMISSION GRANTED

What if? What if those deep desires in our hearts are telling us the truth, revealing to us the life we were *meant* to live? After all, God made the masculine heart, set

DISPATCH

I really do want all the things you talked about. I really do want to fight for everything holy and beautiful in my wife! I want more than anything to attain or at least attempt the dreams God has placed in me. I desire to be that William Wallace! I want adventure! I want to be powerful! I want to be the knight that rescues my wife! BUT I FEEL INADEQUATE. I know it's not something that I will immediately overcome, but I will answer the call, the call to the wild!

SPENCE

it within every man, and thereby offers him an *invitation*: Come and live out what I meant you to be. What might it look like for you to live from your "wild" heart?

Wild at Heart is not a book about the seven things a man ought to do to be a nicer guy. It is a book about the recovery and release of your heart, your passions, your true nature, which you have been given by God. It's an invitation to rush the fields at Bannockburn, to go west, to leap from the falls and save the Beauty. For if you are going to know who you truly are *as a man*, if you're going to find a life worth living, if you are going to love a woman deeply and not pass on your confusion to your children, you simply must get your heart back. You must head up into the high country of the soul, into wild and uncharted regions and track down that elusive prey.

On a scale of 1 to 10, how badly do you want to be that man and live that life? Why'd you pick that number?

O Lord, open wide the eyes of my soul that I might see the true yearnings of my heart. Uncover my desire for adventure, battle, and beauty. Begin to dismantle all the messages that have challenged and assaulted your design of me. May your invitation to life as a man be forever before me. I accept the invitation to live from my deep heart. Father, use the words of this book and the meditations of my heart to guide, shape, and direct me in this journey that I might be the man you designed me to be. I ask this in the name of Jesus.

THE WILD ONE WHOSE IMAGE WE BEAR

This is a stem
Of that victorious stock; and let us fear
The native mightiness and fate of him.

HENRY V

BEFORE SETTING OUT

Again, I'm going to urge you to do three things before you start working through this chapter:

If it's been more than a week since you read chapter 2 of *Wild at Heart*, you'll want to reread it to get back into it. (Get outside if you can—for that, and for the work you're doing here.)

Second, it would be a very good idea to watch *Braveheart*—even if you've seen it dozens of times. For those of you reluctant to view it, I might note that I don't especially enjoy the violent scenes myself, but they are predictable and you can let them pass by or fast-forward. The film raises some crucial questions for men, and, perhaps more importantly than that, offers a powerful picture of Jesus Christ, who gave himself for the freedom of his people. Watch it on Saturday night, and then compare your experience with church the next morning.

Third, spend a few moments looking through some photos of your father. The reason will become clear as you work through the journey below.

GUT REACTION

Before we continue the quest, jot down your gut reaction to this chapter. How did it strike you? Did anything stir you, get your blood going? Did anything grab you, frustrate you, make you mad? Was there a major "aha!," a revelation of some kind? Again, don't edit your thoughts to make them sound "spiritual" or "manly" or whatever. (Use the Field Notes on page 40 to record your thoughts.)

GETTING YOUR BEARINGS

The Goal

Early in this chapter I said, "A man has to know where he comes from, and what he's made of." Those are two of the deepest questions of the masculine soul—even if we may not always be aware of them—and they are linked. What a man thinks he's made of is so often shaped by what he thinks his father is made of. As the old saying goes, "The fruit doesn't fall far from the tree." Yet we are something more than our father's son . . . we bear the image of God. What does *that* mean? Perhaps in finding his wild heart we might find our own.

Trail Markers

- You must know where you come from, and what you're made of.
- But a father—even a good one—is never enough to fully and finally answer that question.
- This yearning for a battle to fight is deep in the heart of God.
- He, too, longs for adventure and risk—far more than we.
- And he has a Beauty to love, whom he pursues with amazing passion.
- This is the victorious stock from which you come.

SETTING OUT

If a boy is to become a man, if a man is to know he is one, this is not an option. A man *has* to know where he comes from, and what he's made of.

It would be helpful to take a moment or two and think about your father, the kind of man he is, or was. What was your father's occupation? What did he like to do?

What was he like emotionally? Was he full of fun, or was he serious, or even gloomy? Did he have a good sense of humor?

What about his temper? How did he handle his anger?

How did he tend to deal with troubles and adversity?

FROM THE MAP

Listen to me, you who
    pursue righteousness
    and who seek the LORD:
Look to the rock from which
    you were cut
    and to the quarry from
    which you were hewn . . .

ISAIAH 51:1

What was your father's great battle or battles? Was he a man with a deep sense of personal mission? If so, for what? If not, why not?

Would you say he was a man of deep courage? What other word would you use if not courageous? Fierce? Hesitant? Timid?

Did he ever tell you about any of his adventures as a young man, or about his life as a bachelor?

Was your father a man who lived life as a great adventure, a man willing to take risks?

What was his courtship of your mother like? How did they meet and fall in love? Have you seen him rescue the Beauty?

DISPATCH

I am a really nice guy who lost his heart in his childhood. I grew up in a Christian home with a dad who was basically a dry alcoholic, living sports through me from fifth grade all the way through high school.

GEORGE

How would you characterize your father? Choose five or ten words that come to mind when you think of him as a man. (Be really honest—no one needs to read this but you.)

Example: Tender, funny, loving, strong, generous, daring
            or
            Distant, sullen, withdrawn, fearful, addicted, angry

Which of your father's attributes do you think you inherited?[1]

On page 21 of *Wild at Heart* I told the briefest account about how my friend Craig came to realize that his real father was a hero, a warrior, a man sold out for God. I said that when he took his father's true name back, he "took back a much more noble identity" and "a much more dangerous place in the story." Is that what you feel you've been given by your father? What if you overheard your closest friends talking about you, and they said, "He's just like his dad"—how would that make you feel? Why?

Would it thrill you to be introduced as a "chip off the old block"? If not, can you think of a few words to describe the father you *wish* you had? Is there an image of him in film or story . . . or in a man you know?

---

[1] Many of these good questions came from or were inspired by a book titled *Recording Your Family History* by William Fletcher (New York: Dodd, Mead and Company, 1986).

WHAT ABOUT JESUS?

I know, it almost sounds too spiritual. In a man's search for his strength, telling him that he's made in the image of God may not sound like a whole lot of encouragement at first. To most men, God is either distant or he is weak—the very thing they'd report of their earthly fathers. It's true that our image of God as Father is profoundly shaped by the father we knew (or didn't know) as a child. Copy here the five or ten words you used above to summarize your father. Which of those words feel true to you about God—especially as he relates to you? Circle them.

And what about Jesus? He came, after all, to make the hidden God known (John 1:18). In Jesus we have a perfect picture of God (Hebrews 1:3). Be honest now—what is your image of Jesus *as a man*?

If you grew up in a religious home, or perhaps attended Sunday school, can you recall some of the early pictures you saw of Jesus? If so, describe the man portrayed there. Is he "gentle Jesus, meek and mild"? Or is he the fierce Lion of Judah?

What would *you* have said to answer the question "Is Jesus more like Mother Teresa or William Wallace?"

Another way of getting at our true thoughts of God is by asking the question "What is godliness?" You hear everyone at your church describe some guy as "a real godly man." What comes to mind about him? What do you assume he'll be like when you meet him?

What would you have to conclude about Jesus from the men in your church? For example, how do they handle controversy—especially the leadership? Do they tiptoe around it? Or do they walk right into the hornet's nest, as Jesus did, and turn some tables over in the temple? Do they live with adventure? What have they done with the Beauty?

I said you can tell what kind of man you've got simply by noting the impact he has on you. Does he make you bored? Does he scare you with his doctrinal Nazism? Does he make you want to scream because he's just so very nice? What's it like to hang around with the men in your church? What is their impact on you? And what do you feel you ought to do or be when you're around them?

WARNING!

I want to draw a distinction between *nice* and *kind*. I'm using *nice* here to mean a passive, sweet, two-dimensional man who never, ever rocks the boat. But I don't mean to suggest that a godly man is therefore rude, or belligerent, or unable to be tender. Jesus could be fierce . . . or immensely kind, depending on what was needed.

BRAVEHEART INDEED

How would you say Jesus of Nazareth is like William Wallace as portrayed in *Braveheart*? (See A Break in the Clouds below and on page 48.) And, how are they different in your mind?

"The Lord is a Gentleman." Have you heard that phrase, or one like it? Do you think it's accurate, as in, *Is Jesus mostly concerned with good manners and with his reputation?*

Compare your experience to watching *Braveheart* at the Battle of Stirling with, say, the Sunday morning service at your church.

A BREAK IN THE CLOUDS

If you haven't seen the film *Braveheart*, or even if you have, I recommend watching it again as part of your work here. In particular, I want you to see the scene that leads up to the Battle of Stirling, which I quote from in this chapter. It's just fascinating in its parallels to the words of Christ. Wallace comes to the field of Stirling to find the Scots losing heart. The Pharisees (the nobles) do not know how to give a man back his heart. But Wallace does.

First, he gives them an identity—he calls them "Sons of Scotland." It might help to remember that the Scots were the only people the Romans could not conquer. After losing battle upon battle against the Scots, the Romans finally built Hadrian's Wall simply to keep them out of the empire. So in calling them Sons of Scotland, Wallace gives them a noble identity and a much more dangerous place in the story.

Then Wallace forces them to face the reality that a life lived in fear is not a life worth living. The words are hauntingly similar to Christ when he says, "What will it profit a man if he gains the whole world, and loses his own soul [his heart]?" (Mark 8:36 NKJV).

Think back to some of the pictures you've seen of Jesus on Sunday school walls, or perhaps in certain Bibles. Is the man depicted there someone you would follow into battle, or into an adventure, or come alongside as you rescue the Beauty?

GOD'S BATTLE TO FIGHT

Remember that wild man, Samson? He's got a pretty impressive masculine résumé: killed a lion with his bare hands, pummeled and stripped thirty Philistines when they used his wife against him, and finally, after they burned her to death, he killed a thousand men with the jawbone of a donkey. Not a guy to mess with. But did you notice? All those events happened when "the *Spirit of the* LORD came powerfully upon him" (Judges 15:14, emphasis added).

WARNING!

I'm very aware that the notion of a fierce God is hitting two audiences in the wrong way. There are certain men who seem to gravitate toward the picture of a wrathful God, ready to bring judgment on the unrighteous. I had dinner with such a man recently, and he scared me. Bubbling just beneath the surface of a Christian veneer he seemed angry, violent. I found nothing good in his God at all. Really, his God seemed just plain mean.

On the other hand, I know many men, gentle and artistic, who pull away from a God of strength in order to favor a God of mercy. And while I appreciate the sensitive nature of these men and their God, I always feel that something is missing, something brave and intentional.

How do you think a man would act if the Spirit of God got hold of him? Does Samson immediately come to mind? Why or why not?

I quoted Tremper Longman (from a book called *Bold Love*) saying, "Virtually every book of the Bible—Old and New Testaments—and almost every page tells us about God's warring activity." Have you seen the Bible that way—as an account of a great battle that God himself is fighting?

FROM THE MAP

When God delivers his people out of the bondage of Egypt, Pharaoh doesn't just roll over and take it. He sends his entire army on chariots to slaughter the fleeing slaves—including the women and children. Let's pick up the story there:

> Then Moses stretched out his hand over the sea, and all that night the LORD drove the sea back with a strong east wind and turned it into dry land. The waters were divided, and the Israelites went through the sea on dry ground, with a wall of water on their right and on their left.
>
> The Egyptians pursued them, and all Pharaoh's horses and chariots and horsemen followed them into the sea . . .
>
> Then the LORD said to Moses, "Stretch out your hand over the sea so that the waters may flow back over the Egyptians and their chariots and horsemen . . . and the LORD swept them into the sea. The water flowed back and covered the chariots and horsemen—the entire army of Pharaoh that

had followed the Israelites into the sea. Not one of them survived (Exodus 14:21–23, 26–28).

It is after this battle that the Israelites cheered, "The LORD is a warrior; the LORD is his name" (Exodus 15:3).

This story from Exodus is just one among hundreds given to us in the Bible to reveal the warring activity of God. There are the great battles of King David; Elijah against the prophets of Baal; Jesus taking on the hypocrites, kicking out demons, and finally wrestling the keys of hell and death away from Satan. Would you gather from all this that God's nature is basically passive or aggressive?

And what *is* God's great battle to fight? Is it, as some churches seem to convey, simply to get people to stop sinning? Or perhaps to silence heretics? In your own words, what is God fighting *for*?

Read Revelation 19:11–21. How does Jesus return at the end of the age, and how does he bring an end to this chapter of his story?

A BREAK IN THE CLOUDS

"If you have any doubts as to whether or not God loves wildness, spend a night in the woods . . . alone. Take a walk out in a thunderstorm. Go for a swim with a pod of killer whales. Get a bull moose mad at you. Whose idea was this, anyway? The Great Barrier Reef with its great white sharks, the jungles of India with their tigers, the deserts of the Southwest with all those rattlesnakes—would you describe them as 'nice' places? Most of the earth is not safe; but it's good."

We normally try to avoid weather and wildness. But I suggest you do just the opposite—spend an evening out in the wild, alone and without a flashlight. Or, if a storm hits, go out in it. (My boys and I do that on summer nights when a howling thunderstorm comes in over the Rockies. We especially love the wind.) Ask yourself, *What is this telling me about the wild heart of God?*

GOD'S ADVENTURE TO LIVE

After our foray into grizzly country, it then occurred to me that after God made this dangerous world, he pronounced it *good*, for heaven's sake. It's his way of letting us know he rather prefers adventure, danger, risk, the element of surprise. This whole creation is unapologetically *wild*. God loves it that way. You can learn a great deal about a man by the kind of world he builds for himself. For example, consider the professor who seals himself off from all human contact in the safety of his books, or the millionaire who has his servants emboss his toilet paper. What does the world God made tell you about his likes, his personality? What do you learn about God's heart from a place like the outback of Australia, or the open ocean of the North Atlantic?

But what about his own life? We know he has a battle to fight—but does God have an *adventure* to live? I mean, he already knows everything that's going to happen, right? How could there be any risk to his life; hasn't he got everything under absolute control? What have you been taught about the risk-taking nature of God?

If we're honest I think most of us would have to admit that we try to reduce the element of risk in our lives. On a scale of 1 to 10, rate your willingness to take risks (a) at work and (b) in your relationships.

Now, rate God's willingness to risk in his work and his relationships—keeping in mind the story from Genesis where God turns over the care of creation to Adam and Eve, and also gives them freedom to reject him, knowing that if they do, they'll plunge the whole world into evil.

And now recall that universal trait in little boys, who want to be the hero of some great and daring quest. Can you see something of the heart of God reflected there? As I wrote, "Do you know why God loves writing such incredible stories? Because *he loves to come through*. He loves to show us that he has what it takes." Wouldn't you love to show the world that you have what it takes?

GOD'S BEAUTY TO LOVE

I said that God's wildness and his fierceness are inseparable from his romantic heart. Romantic? Would you have said that God is *romantic*?

WARNING!

This might be the most difficult "new thought" many men encounter—the idea that God has set up even his own life to involve immense risk. There's a rather heated debate right now over "open theism," and I'm not entering into that here. In saying that God has an adventure to live, I don't mean the world is chaotic, or out of control, or that somehow God's sovereignty is diminished. Far from it. Only a truly amazing God could set this world in motion and still never lose control. After all, doesn't he walk "on the wings of the wind" (Psalm 104:3 NKJV)? Could that be boring?

Whose idea was it to create the human form in such a way that a kiss could be so delicious? And he didn't stop there, as only lovers know. Starting with her eyes, King Solomon is feasting on his beloved through the course of their wedding night. He loves her hair, her smile, her lips "drop sweetness as the honeycomb" and "milk and honey are under your tongue." How does Solomon know *that*?

For some reason, most men never attribute the wonders of sex to God, that the whole delicious mystery of intercourse from foreplay to orgasm was his idea. But of course, it was. Let's say sex has never been invented. Then, one day, some guy comes up with the idea. What kind of person would you expect him to be—what kind of person would have invented sex?

Two questions: First, would such an erotic and scandalous book have been placed in the Bible by the Christians you know? And second, what kind of God would put the Song of Songs in the canon of holy Scripture?

FROM THE MAP

I quoted a section of the Song of Songs, one in which King Solomon and his bride were making love from the top down. Let's look at a later passage, where this passionate man is appreciatively working his way *up* his beloved:

Your graceful legs are like jewels,
    the work of a craftsman's hands.
Your navel is a rounded goblet
    that never lacks blended wine. [Again, how does
    he know *that*?]
Your waist is a mound of wheat
    encircled by lilies. [Meaning, a *feast*] . . .
How beautiful you are and how pleasing,
    O love, with your delights!

Your stature is like that of the palm,
    and your breasts like clusters of fruit.
I said, "I will climb the palm tree;
    I will take hold of its fruit." [Whoa now!]

SONG OF SONGS 7:1–2, 6–8

Down through the centuries the church has understood the Song of Songs to be both a celebration of passion in marriage *and* a metaphor for Christ and his bride. Think about how much you want sex with a beautiful woman. How does *that* reflect the image of God?

God has a bride; we know that from Scripture. What lengths will he go to in order to rescue her? For example, how long has he given pursuit? And, does he play it safe with his own life?

THE INEVITABLE CONCLUSION

This is our true Father, the stock from which the heart of every man is drawn. From which your heart is drawn.

What if you were an orphan, and you had never known your true father? What if you then somehow learned the truth—that your father was in fact a hero of some kind, a fighter pilot, the most decorated man in his squadron, who shot down dozens of planes single-handedly, and how after the war he became a renowned explorer given some of the most daring challenges known to man, and furthermore it was widely known that he had gone undercover behind the Iron Curtain to rescue one of the most beautiful women in the world, and married her, and you are their son?

On top of that, what if it was said by those who knew your father well that you truly are his son, a chip off the old block?

I've noticed that so often our word to boys is *don't*. Don't climb on that, don't break anything, don't be so aggressive, don't be so noisy, don't be so messy, don't take such crazy risks. But God's design—which he placed in boys as the picture of himself—is a resounding YES. Be fierce, be wild, be passionate. Now what words would you use to describe "a godly man"?

A BREAK IN THE CLOUDS

You'll recall the quote I used at the top of the chapter, about someone being a "stem" of some "victorious stock," and that everyone should beware of him, "fear the native mightiness and fate of him." These lines are from Shakespeare's play *Henry V*. Here's the context: Henry, a young king only recently come to the throne of England, has been incited to war against France. He warned them that he would not hesitate to invade on just grounds, that he has a better and more historical claim to the throne than their current king (a frail old politician). The young French princes mock Henry's threats . . . and he invades. Still, the French nobles think they have nothing to fear from this young upstart of a would-be king.

But then the old French monarch, whose memory is better than theirs, reminds them that Henry "is bred out of that bloody strain that haunted us in our familiar [past]. Witness our too much memorable shame" when in 1346 Edward III of

England and his son, Edward the Black Prince, dealt them a devastating blow at the Battle of Crecy.

> And all our princes captiv'd by the hand
> Of that black name, Edward, Black Prince of Wales.

He remembers that Edward III stood on a hilltop and watched his son, the prince, whom the French king calls his "heroical seed," do terrible feats of victory on the battlefield, and drive all his enemies before him. And then he reminds them that this young king, this Henry who now invades their country,

> . . . is a stem
> Of that victorious stock; and let us fear
> The native mightiness and fate of him. (Act II, Scene IV)

That's what it means to be called a son of God.

Lord, you are more passionate and more fierce than I ever imagined. Open my eyes, show me your true nature, and show me your nature in me. I want your work in my life—O make me free, alive to fight the battles you bring me, to live the adventure, to love the beauty. Do this work in my soul, I pray, dear Christ. Amen.

THE QUESTION THAT HAUNTS EVERY MAN

Are you there?
Say a prayer for the Pretender
Who started out so young and strong
Only to surrender

JACKSON BROWNE
"The Pretender" © 1976 by Swallow Turn Music

BEFORE SETTING OUT

Again, three things before you start working through this chapter:

Reread chapter 3 if it's not fresh in your heart and mind.

Second, it would be a really good idea to watch *Legends of the Fall*. The three sons—Alfred, Tristan, and Samuel—and their father, Colonel Ludlow, offer four archetypal models of different kinds of men. Again, I don't love everything about this movie, but it is a very powerful story about the masculine journey, good and bad.

Third, look at some family photos of yourself as an adult, including pictures from the last couple of years. Also, if you have an audio or even better, some video of yourself, have a look at that. What kind of man is pictured there?

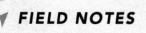 **FIELD NOTES**

or

Stand buck naked in front of a mirror for ten minutes. What's your reaction to be faced with yourself? (What's your reaction to this assignment!?)

GUT REACTION

As always, I think it's best to start with a gut reaction to the chapter. What really struck you? What did it make you want to go do? (Use the Field Notes on page 65 to record your thoughts.)

GETTING YOUR BEARINGS

The Goal

This chapter takes you into some naked self-assessment. Something's gone wrong in men, and we know it. Something about us, or in us, is just not what we know it was meant to be. What's *happened* to us? Why aren't we more fierce, daring, and passionate? You're going to need to be really honest—brutally honest—if you hope to continue the journey from here. Remember, we have to cross the desert, the no-man's-land, before winning the promised land.

Trail Markers

- The world is filled with caricatures of masculinity—posers—but very few real men.

- And every one of us posers shares a deepest fear: to be found out, exposed as an impostor.
- The reason, in part, goes back to Adam's fall—and the way every man since him has fallen.
- So men handle that by becoming either violent (driven) or retreating (passive)—we mishandle our strength.

SETTING OUT

A man is fierce . . . passionate . . . wild at heart? You wouldn't know it from what normally walks around in a pair of trousers. If that's true, how come there are so many lonely women, so many fatherless children, so few men around? Why is it that the world seems filled with "caricatures" of masculinity? How come when men look in their hearts they don't discover something valiant and dangerous, but instead find anger, lust, and fear? Most of the time, I feel more fearful than I do fierce. Why is that?

OUR STRUGGLES

Without a great battle in which a man can live or die, the fierce part of our nature goes underground and just sort of stews there in an anger that seems to have no reason. Are you aware of a simmering anger down under the surface of your life? How do you react when somebody cuts you off on the highway? How about when your children openly dismiss or ignore you? What goes on inside when you're criticized at work, or when some project you're doing breaks apart in your hands?

FROM THE MAP

I don't really understand myself, for I want to do what is right, but I don't do it.

ROMANS 7:15 NLT

Describe a recent event that really made you mad. What happened?

A BREAK IN THE CLOUDS

You may not be aware of anger because in the church we tend to hide it, drive it underground. Henri Nouwen called it "frozen anger":

> Anger in particular seems close to a professional vice in the contemporary ministry. Pastors are angry at their leaders for not leading and at their followers for not following. They are angry at those who do not come to church for not coming and angry at those who do come for coming without enthusiasm. They are angry at their families, who make them feel guilty, and angry at themselves for not being who they want to be. This is not an open, blatant, roaring anger, but an anger hidden behind the smooth word, the smiling face, and the polite handshake. It is a frozen anger . . .

THE WAY OF THE HEART

Have you enjoyed thinking about getting even with someone, or giving your boss a piece of your mind, or maybe taking out your "frustration" in a destructive way?

WARNING!

Anger is not necessarily a bad thing, by the way. Paul says, "Be angry, and do not sin . . ." (Ephesians 4:26 NKJV), which makes it clear that anger and sin are not one and the same, that it's possible to be angry in a righteous way. Furthermore, I think anger is a good sign—at least there's something still alive inside, something that would love to fight back.

Have you done something angry or destructive? Perhaps it's veiled in the form of destructive tendencies in your life—maybe even against yourself—like a habit that's destroying your health.

Why are so many men addicted to sports? It's the biggest adventure many of us ever taste. Why do so many others lose themselves in their career? Same reason. How about gambling, or the guys who spend hours online, e-trading stocks? There's a taste of excitement and risk to it, no question. And who's to blame them? The rest of their life is chores and tedious routine. It's no coincidence that many men fall into an affair not for love, not even for sex, but, by their own admission, for adventure. Where do you go for a taste of adventure these days? Do you spend a lot of free time in front of the TV, or at work, or down at the gym? Has a hobby become more of an obsession? What might the balance on your credit cards say about where you are looking for adventure?

And where do you feel *pulled* to go for a thrill, even if you haven't given in?

Last, what about lust—how's it going there? How strong is the lure of a beautiful woman, or a sexual fantasy these days? Have you found yourself lingering a little too long over a woman who is not your wife?

When is your struggle with lust or pornography or masturbation the strongest? Can you connect it to disappointment, stress, or pressure at work or at home?

I hope you're getting the picture by now. If a man does not find those things for which his heart is made, if he is never even invited to live for them from his heart, he will look for them in some other way. This is such a key thought. *We will never get past our struggles and addictions until we recover the true heart and true life we were meant for.*

OUR FEAR

Because we bear the image of God in our strength, because we are a "stem of that victorious stock," there's one thing we all know: We are made to *come through*. And yet we wonder, *Can I? Will I? When the going gets rough, when it really matters, can I really pull it off?* That is why every man shares the same core fear of being exposed, being "found out," that something will happen and he'll be revealed to be an impostor, and not really a man. Are you aware of that fear? Where would you hate to be called upon to come through, because you don't know whether or not you *can* come through?

It's time for some candid self-assessment. How do you measure up as a man? In response to the following questions, I want you to write a simple, candid description of yourself *as a man*. (You don't need to show this to anyone.)

I mentioned the film *Legends of the Fall*, how every man who's seen it wants to be Tristan—but most see themselves as Alfred or Samuel. If you watched *Legends*, who do you see yourself as—Alfred, Tristan, Samuel, or their father, Colonel Ludlow? Why? Has it always been that way?

I've talked to many men about the film *Braveheart* and though every single one of them would love to be William Wallace, the dangerous warrior-hero, most see themselves as Robert the Bruce, the weak, intimidated guy who keeps folding under pressure. How about you—would you say you live more like William Wallace or Robert the Bruce? Why?

I'd love to think of myself as Indiana Jones, but I'm afraid I'm more like Woody Allen. Is there another character you do see yourself as, or fear you might in fact be?

DISPATCH

The movie *City Slickers* is a wry comedy about a man who has lost his heart. Billy Crystal plays Mitch, a thirty-nine-year-old ad executive for a radio station who has recently been stripped of any real authority he had at work. The next day he's invited in to his son's classroom for "Career Day." His son is so embarrassed by his dad that he tries at first to tell the class that his dad is a submarine commander. Crystal takes the stage to deliver this depressing monologue:

Value this time in your life, kids. 'Cause this is the time in your life when you still have your choices. And it goes by so fast. When you're a teenager you think you can do anything, and you do. Your twenties are a blur. Thirties . . . you raise your family, you make a little money, and you think to yourself, "What happened to my twenties?" Forties? You grow a little potbelly . . . you grow another chin. The music starts to get too loud . . . one of your old girlfriends from high school becomes a grandmother. Fifties, you have a minor surgery. You'll call it a "procedure," but it's a surgery. Sixties . . . you'll have a *major* surgery, the music is still loud but it doesn't matter because you can't hear it anyway. The seventies, you and the wife retire to Fort Lauderdale. You start eating dinner at two o'clock in the afternoon . . . you have lunch around ten . . . breakfast the night before. You spend most of your time wandering around malls looking for the ultimate soft yogurt and muttering, "How come the kids don't call? How come the kids don't call?" The

eighties, you'll have a major stroke. Ya end up babbling to some Jamaican nurse who your wife can't stand, but who you call "Mama." Any questions?
How sadly true.

Let's take the battle: How well are you fighting these days? Do you live with courage for the most part? What are you fighting over, if anything?

What battles do you *not* want to face? Where are you hanging back in your life, not really and fully jumping in? Is it tough situations at work, or at home with your wife and children? What about with men working on cars, or the guys down at the gym? Where are you avoiding exposure?

Where are you holding back from diving into a situation that's murky and potentially painful?

WARNING!

Two thoughts as you enter into what may be your first really candid picture of yourself as a man . . . First, this isn't the end of the story. We're only in chapter 3, and if there weren't hope for us posers I wouldn't have written this book. The whole promise of the Beatitudes is that anybody under any condition can enter the transforming kingdom of God. Allow me a paraphrase: Blessed are the posers, for they shall be valiant warriors.

Second, this isn't going to be helpful if you inflate your grade here so as to sound like a better guy than you really are; nor is it helpful to assume a false Christian humility and intentionally lower your marks because that's the "spiritual" thing to do. God desires truth in our inmost being, says David in Psalm 51. Be honest—no more, no less.

If you were called into a real battle tomorrow, would you step forward to lead the charge, knowing beyond doubt that you *are* powerful and dangerous?

How about real adventure, not imitation stuff: Are you living with risk and daring, or do you play it safe more often than not?

Write a list of "my worst fears," the things you hope and pray you are never called upon to do or to lead. Why do you fear them?

If you were swept up into a real Adventure, would you leap with confidence into it, knowing beyond doubt that you have what it takes?

And as for the Beauty—are you fighting for her heart? How often do you talk to her at an intimate level? Do you often ask her how she thinks the two of you are doing? Have you ever asked her that?

Do you know you have the passionate strength to win her . . . not just once, but to keep winning her? Has the woman in your life ever told you that she is so grateful for how you've loved her?

Really—how do you see yourself as a man? Are words like *strong, passionate,* and *dangerous* words you would choose?

Do you have the courage to ask those in your life what they think of you as a man? What words do you fear they would choose?

◄ FIELD NOTES

WARNING!

It may be next to impossible to get this kind of feedback. A woman who looked at these questions told us, "I don't think I could be that honest with my husband." I'll say a whole lot more about approaching your wife for feedback in chapter 10.

Remember back in chapter 2 I said that you can tell what kind of man you've got simply by noting the impact he has on you. Does he make you bored? Does he scare you with his doctrinal Nazism? Does he make you want to scream because he's just so very nice? What do you think *your* impact is on others? What do you fear it is?

Put yourself in the question I asked on page 17 of *Wild at Heart*. Let's say a group of men you respect and women you admire are talking about you. What are they going to say—that you are a really sweet guy, or that you are a dangerous and powerful man?

A BREAK IN THE CLOUDS

Okay, I have a mission for you. But it may be the bravest thing you've ever done . . . and the most life-changing. Ask a few people who know you well—your wife, your older children, a friend or colleague—to give you some feedback about you *as a man*. It's hard to get an honest and candid reply, especially if they are not used to being asked for such information. You might explain that you're working through some frank self-assessment, and ask them to answer you in writing, as a start.

Input from a few key men in your life	Input from the woman in your life

What am I like to work with, or be a friend to, or go to church with? How would you describe me as a man?
 	
Am I the kind of man . . .
    you would follow into battle?
    you would invite on an expedition?
    you would want as a business partner?
    you would seek advice from on your marriage or on raising your children?
    you would want to listen to for hours on spiritual matters?
Am I one of the best men you know?
	What am I like to live with?
	
	Do you feel invited to share your heart with me, and would you feel safe doing so, confident that I would handle your heart well?
	
	Do you feel pursued by me—that I am truly fighting for you?
	
	Has our marriage turned out to be what you had hoped for as a young woman?
	
	Do you look forward to sex with me?

ADAM AND HIS SONS

God gave Adam a noble mission, a mission that is still written into the heart of every man, in the form of his desires. What is that mission, in your own words?

And how does it make you feel to realize what God did *not* tell Adam about the unfolding story, and the test that was about to come?

Was that a new revelation to you—that Adam was standing right there when Eve was being tempted, and *he didn't do a thing*? How did that strike you, realizing that's what happened?

Does Adam's sin help you understand the way men nowadays sin—and, more importantly, can you see that same dynamic working in your own life? When have you been paralyzed in a situation you didn't know how to handle or didn't think you could handle? When have you been silent when you really should have spoken up?

AND EVE?

Your woman is fallen as well, of course. We all are. But women sin differently from men. They tend to hide their vulnerability and become hard, or independent, or controlling women—or, on the other hand, they become desperately needy and overly submissive, "never raise their voice" kind of women (who, by the way, are also not being vulnerable). How does your woman handle her vulnerability? Do you ever feel controlled by her, or does she sometimes feel clingy?

What about her beauty—does she hide it behind efficiency and working hard and being "spiritual"? Or perhaps she handles her insecurity there by trying extra hard, spending a lot of time in front of the mirror in the morning, dieting, talking a lot about her weight, and the like. How invited do you feel by her? Is *alluring* a word that characterizes your woman most of the time?

And thinking about the above, how strong do you feel when your wife is not doing well, or when you are faced with her sin? Do you feel like a man around her?

POSERS

Adam (and every man with him, I might add) has blown it, and he knows that something has gone wrong within him, that he is no longer what he was meant to be. It's not just that he makes a bad decision; he *gives away* something essential to his nature. He is marred now; his strength is fallen and he knows it. Then what happens? Adam hides. "I was afraid because I was naked; so I hid" (Genesis 3:10). You don't need a course in psychology to understand men. Understand that verse, let its implications sink in, and the men around you will suddenly come into focus. We are hiding, every last one of us. Well aware that we, too, are not what we were meant to be, desperately afraid of exposure, terrified of being seen for what we are and are not, we have run off into the bushes. We hide in our office, at the gym, behind the newspaper, and mostly behind our personality. Most of what you encounter when you meet a man is a facade, an elaborate fig leaf, a brilliant disguise.

Describe your personality:

Now—how does it work for you? What do people never ask you to do?

Any day now, I'll be found out is a pretty common theme among us guys. Truth be told, most of us are faking our way through life. We pick only those battles we are sure to win, only those adventures we are sure to handle, only those beauties we are sure to love. Are you aware of that fear, that one day you'll be "found out"? What is it you are afraid people are going to see about you as a man?

Have you had a nightmare like the one I shared, being onstage without a clue as to what's going on, or like the one my friend had about the FBI closing in on him? How does yours go? What do you think it's saying about a fear of your own?

DISPATCH

As I flipped through your book, the Jackson Browne quote that leads off chapter 3 put me on my knees sobbing. I know that album inside and out, but I never thought I was the Pretender. Oh, God, I am the Pretender!

PETER

I offered two basic categories for how a fallen man handles his strength: violent men and retreating men. Violent men are the guys who are overcompensating, running extra hard at life, giving 150 percent. Sometimes they are simply perfectionists and workaholics; others are actually violent. They are *striving* in various ways to prove that they are a man, or at least, to never be exposed.

Retreating men are passive men, the ultimate nice guys—they never make a fuss, are eager to help, but hang back and hide behind their desk, or a newspaper, or even a veneer of Christian spirituality. They basically live to avoid the question and stay away from any possible exposure. Which of the two categories do you put yourself in . . . and why? Can you give a few examples, maybe one from home and one from work?

I've borrowed the following list from some thoughts by Dr. Larry Crabb. How do you see yourself (why don't you circle each one that applies to you)?

A man who is NOT living well	A man who IS living well
Is easily discouraged by defeat/setbacks	Survives the down times with confidence
Is especially weak in the face of sexual temptation	Feels a growing strength to resist temptation
Demands attention and support / needs to be taken care of	Enjoys encouragement but never requires it

A man who is NOT living well	A man who IS living well
Is not easily criticized	Responds thoughtfully to criticism
Is unapproachable on an intimate level	Welcomes and invites deep conversations
Views life as a problem to solve: "I need a plan to follow"	Views life as a mystery to enter: "I need a God to trust"
Sees God as impersonal (a source of principles)	Sees God as a person to grow more intimate with
Makes you doubt that you could count on him to come through	Conveys a core strength that you know you can count on

The evidence is clear: Adam and Eve's fall sent a tremor through the human race. A fatal flaw entered the original, and it's been passed on to every son and daughter. Thus, every little boy and every little girl comes into the world set up for a loss of heart. Even if he can't quite put it into words, every man is haunted by the question, "Am I really a man? Have I got what it takes . . . when it counts?"

Are you a bit more aware now of that Question in your own heart and life?

DISPATCH

I never had my masculinity validated. I never learned my identity. I lived my life like a robot, knowing how to perform and do the right thing . . . always, but with no emotion. As Leanne Payne puts it, I've been "walking beside myself" just about my entire life. I always felt like I was on the outside looking in. I took on this tough image as a child, but always felt this big question mark stamped across my chest.

PRESTON

Search me, O God, and know my heart. Try me and know my fearful thoughts. Reveal to me the ways I pose and hide, and O God, lead me in the everlasting way, the way of truth and strength. May I live with passion and zeal, may my soul be captured by you for something big, noble, and worthy of your kingdom. Remove the quiet desperation of my soul, chase away resignation, anger, and the addictions I run to. Free me to be a strong, passionate, and dangerous man . . . as you created me to be. Draw me beyond the battles I know I can win, lure me to larger adventures . . . speak with power those words I long to hear: "You have what it takes." I ask all this in Jesus' name.

CHAPTER 4

THE WOUND

In the clearing stands a boxer
And a fighter by his trade
And he carries the reminder
Of every glove that laid him down
and cut him till he cried out
in his anger and his pain,
"I am leaving,
I am leaving,"
But the fighter still remains.

PAUL SIMON
"The Boxer" (© 1968 by Paul Simon)

BEFORE SETTING OUT

I recommend you watch *The Kid*, starring Bruce Willis. I know, it seems like a predictable comedy, but I'm telling you it chronicles the story of a man finding the root of his false self in his father-wound in a very clear way.

Also, if you have some old yearbooks from your school days available to you, I want to suggest a very powerful experiment. Follow your development from a boy to a young man through those photos (or any photos that chronicle the years for you—maybe the annual family Christmas photo). See if you notice any significant changes—especially in the years you received your major wounds. I did this the other night, and I found that in my eighth-grade photo I still look fairly

FIELD NOTES

young and innocent, but that by tenth grade I look sort of blown away, lost, disoriented. And that's when it happened, right in between those years.

GUT REACTION

What's your gut-level reaction to this chapter? What did it stir in you? What did it make you feel? What did it make you want to do?

GETTING YOUR BEARINGS

The Goal

Your goal is simple, but daunting: to uncover your wound. You need to see how you've been wounded, understand where the wound came from, and how it has shaped the way you've lived every day of your life—right up to this moment today.

Trail Markers

- Every boy has two Questions: Do you love me? Do I have what it takes?
- Most men live their lives haunted by the Question, or crippled by the answer they've been given.
- Because masculinity is *bestowed*. A boy learns who is he and what he's got from a man, or the company of men.
- Yet every boy, in his journey to become a man, takes an arrow in the center of his heart, in the place of his strength. And the wound is nearly always given by his father.
- With the wound comes a message, and out of the message we make a vow.
- The result is a false self—a deep uncertainty in the soul, and a driven or passive man on the outside.

89

SETTING OUT

The story of Adam's fall is every man's story. It is simple and straightforward, almost mythic in its brevity and depth. And so every man comes into the world set up for a loss of heart. Then comes the story we are much more aware of—our own story. Where Adam's story seems simple and straightforward, our own seems complex and detailed; many more characters are involved, and the plot is sometimes hard to follow. But the outcome is always the same: a wound in the soul. Every boy, in his journey to become a man, takes an arrow in the center of his heart, in the place of his strength. Because the wound is rarely discussed and even more rarely healed, every man carries a wound. And the wound is nearly always given by his father.

UNDERSTANDING THE MASCULINE JOURNEY

In order to understand how a man receives a wound, you must understand the central truth of a boy's journey to manhood: Masculinity is bestowed. A boy learns who he is and what he's got from a man, or the company of men. He cannot learn it any other place. He cannot learn it from other boys, and he cannot learn it from the world of women. The plan from the beginning of time was that his father would lay the foundation for a young boy's heart and pass on to him that essential knowledge and confidence in his strength. Dad would be the first man in his life, and forever the most important man. Above all, he would answer the Question for his son and give him his name.

I told the story of rock climbing with Sam—how it was for him a test of his strength, one day among many that helped to answer his Question, the question every little boy is asking—"Do I have what it takes?" Can you recall a story like that of your own? Write down a few of yours that you remember. What did it mean for you? (And if you cannot recall any, what does that bring up for you now?)

FROM THE MAP

. . . help me for your name's sake; out of the goodness of your love, deliver me. For I am poor and needy, and my heart is wounded within me.

PSALM 109:21–22

Describe a time in your life when you heard words like those Jesus heard from his Father—"I am deeply proud of you; you have what it takes."

Would you say that your father or another key man, or perhaps the company of men, "actively intervened" on your behalf in order to tell you who you are as a man? Give me an example. Does your example represent many others you could have chosen—or was it an exception?

Over the course of your youth up to young manhood, what were you rewarded for, delighted in because of? Was it grades, or sports, or good morals? Did that really answer The Question for you?

I find that most men live their lives haunted by The Question, or crippled by the answer they've been given. How has life answered The Question for you? Do you have a sense of what that answer was? Describe it—put it into words.

MOTHERS AND SONS

It would be good to explore your relationship with your mother before moving on to Dad more deeply. After all, a boy is brought into the world by his mother, and she is the center of his universe in those first tender months and years. She suckles him, nurtures him, protects him; she sings to him, reads to him, watches over him, as the old saying goes, "like a mother hen." She often names him as well, tender names like "my little lamb," or "Mama's little sweetheart," or even "my little boyfriend."

Describe your relationship with your mother—was it close? Closer than your relationship with your father? Answer that question for three main phases of boyhood:

Preschool years (ages 0–5)

Grade school (ages 6–12)

Middle school and high school (ages 13–18)

DISPATCH

Your book spoke specifically to me as I debated whether to let my somewhat timid ten-year-old son and his friend jump off the two-story-high dock at the lake (while my wife looked on in terror). I believe it was part of his initiation—he was so proud of himself and his emerging manhood that he and his friend repeated the jump about a dozen times!

REGGIE

Did your mother have a pet name for you during any of those years? Perhaps there might have been two very different "names"—one she used when feeling affectionate and the other she used when angry with you. Does she call you either still?

Was your mother a source of mercy and tenderness for you? (This would be a *good* thing, by the way.)

Did your mother allow you to be "dangerous"? Did she, for example, let you play with guns? Ride your bike with no hands? Jump off the high dive? Do risky things?

Many women ask their sons to fill a void in their soul that their husband has left. Was that in any way true of your relationship with her? Was her relationship with you closer than the relationship she had with your father? Did she tell you secrets, discuss her life struggles, and even her struggle with your father with you? How did that make you feel?

There comes a time in every young man's life when he leaves his mother's side and enters the world of men, starting with his father's world. How was your separation from your mom? Did she let you go willingly, encourage you to move into your father's world? Did she make it difficult? Did she even understand?

What is your relationship like with her today, as compared to your relationship with your dad? Who do you go to talk to about your life?

FROM FATHER TO SON

Masculinity is an *essence* that is hard to articulate but that a boy naturally craves just as he craves food and water. It is something passed between men. "The traditional way of raising sons," notes Robert Bly, "which lasted for thousands and thousands of years, amounted to fathers and sons living in close—murderously close—proximity, while the father taught the son a trade: perhaps farming or carpentry or blacksmithing or tailoring." My father taught me to fish. We would spend long days together, out in a boat on a lake, trying to catch fish. I will never, ever forget his delight in me when I'd hook one. But the fish were never really the important thing. It was the delight, the contact, the masculine presence gladly bestowing itself on me. "Atta boy, Tiger! Bring him in! That's it . . . well done!"

What are some of your favorite memories together with your dad? *Why* are they favorite memories?

"When a father and son spend long hours together," says Bly, "we could say that a substance almost like food passes from the older body to the younger." This is why my boys loved to wrestle with me—why any healthy boy wants the same with his father. They loved the physical contact, to brush against my cheek, feel the sandpaper of my whiskers, my strength all around them, and to test theirs on me. Do you recall this longing? Did you wrestle with your dad? Was there regular, warm contact with him?

And are you comfortable being physically affectionate with your children?

What did your father teach you to do when you were a boy? Throw a curveball? Fix a car? Paint a landscape? Describe what he passed along to you in the following arenas:

Outdoors

Woodcraft (or some other craft)

Sports

Fighting/self-defense

Women

Finances

God

DISPATCH

I remember my dad worked a lot, even at home. He'd lock himself in his study in the evening, and we had strict orders not to interrupt him. So I would sit outside his study and pass little notes under the door—hoping he would write something back to me. He never did.

DAVID

FIELD NOTES

A BREAK IN THE CLOUDS

I need to clarify two things when it comes to finding our "wound": First, it is not necessarily one clear wound, given on an unforgettable day you remember in detail. Many men can recall the day they received a soul-wound from their father that somehow defined the rest of their relationship with him. But for others, it is an accumulation of subtle wounds and messages, given over time.

Second, I believe that every man carries a wound. No matter how good a man your father was, and may still be, he is not Jesus Christ. Every father is a son of Adam, and every father himself grew up in a world far from Eden. Given these two biblical truths, be very, very cautious to come to the conclusion that you somehow escaped the father-wound. Your father may have repented deeply of his own false self as a young man, and been substantially healed of his own wound before he fathered you. But that is a rare, rare case.

How would you sum up your father's "life lesson" to you? (Examples: *Work hard and you'll get ahead; always look out for Number One; you can't really trust anyone.*)

THE FATHER-WOUND

Every boy, in his journey to become a man, takes an arrow in the center of his heart, in the place of his strength. Because wounds are rarely discussed and even more rarely healed, every man carries a wound. And the wound is nearly always given by his father.

What is your wound? Can you put words to it? Do you remember how it was given—the way it came?

And what was the *message* of that wound—or that series of wounds? What did it say to you about yourself?

FIELD NOTES

DISPATCH

I loved the Disney movie *The Kid*—saw it twice in the theater when it came out because I really identified with the little kid character and his feelings of never doing anything right. I understand now that because of the wound he suffers, he grows up hiding behind his personality—a cold, shallow, "successful" man. I'm every bit as much the Bruce Willis character as I am the little kid.

MATT

In the case of violent fathers, the boy's Question is answered in a devastating way. "Do I have what it takes? Am I a man, Papa?" No, you are a mama's boy, an idiot, a faggot, a seagull. Those are defining sentences that shape a man's life. The assault wounds are like a shotgun blast to the chest. This can get unspeakably evil when it involves physical, sexual, or verbal abuse carried on for years. Violent fathers give a wound that is easier to recognize. How did you experience your father's anger?

What did your father "name" you—what identity did he bestow on you as a boy and young man? Perhaps there might even be an actual name he gave you, like seagull, or fatty, or s#@!head.

The passive wounds are not as obvious. Passive fathers give a blow that is harder to define, because it didn't come as a blow; it came as an absence. Words unspoken, affection withheld . . . As Bly says, "Not receiving any blessing from your father is an injury . . . Not seeing your father when you are small, never being with him, having a remote father, an absent father, a workaholic father, is an injury."

If you still have no clue as to what your wound might be, go to the *effect* of the wound and work backward. Do you live each day with a deep inner strength that comes from knowing you are a real man, that you have what it takes? Or are you a driven man, or a passive man? When did that feeling of drivenness or passivity set in? Did it originate during a certain period in your life?

Another way of getting at the wound is by asking yourself what you are currently working hard at not being discovered as. What arenas are you staying comfortably away from? Why—where did that originate?

A BREAK IN THE CLOUDS

My child arrived just the other day
he came to the world in the usual way—
But there were planes to catch and bills to pay
he learned to walk while I was away
and he was talking 'fore I knew it and as he grew he'd say
"I'm gonna be like you, Dad;
you know I'm gonna be like you."
And the cat's in the cradle and the silver spoon
Little boy blue and the man in the moon
"When you comin' home, Dad?"
"I don't know when,
but we'll get together then—

you know we'll have a good time then."
My son turned 10 just the other day,
He said, "Thanks for the ball, Dad, c'mon, let's play.
Can you teach me to throw?"
I said, "Not today, I got a lot to do."
He said, "That's okay,"
and he walked away but his smile never dimmed;
it said, "I'm gonna be like him, yeah
you know I'm gonna be like him."

"CAT'S IN THE CRADLE,"
SANDY AND HARRY CHAPIN
© 1974; from the Story Songs CD.

THE WOUND'S EFFECT

I think by now you have some idea of the impact your wound has had upon your masculine heart. Much of our life ends up being shaped by it, in one way or another. We take a wound, and with it comes a message, a lie about us and about the world and often about God, too. The wound and lie then lead to a vow, a resolution to never, ever do again whatever it was that might have brought the wound. From that vow we develop a false self.

$$\frac{\text{Wound}}{\text{Lie}} \qquad \text{Vow} \qquad = \qquad \text{False Self}$$

Example:

$$\frac{\text{My father left}}{\text{"You are on your own"}} \qquad \begin{array}{c}\text{I will never trust} \\ \text{anyone again}\end{array} \qquad = \qquad \begin{array}{c}\text{A very independent,} \\ \text{driven man}\end{array}$$

Can you remember making a sort of vow when you were younger—maybe after being wounded? What was that vow?

Can you see that vow affecting you today? As I said, men either overcompensate for their wound and become driven (violent men), or they shrink back and go passive (retreating men). Which would you say is true for you? Is it a little of both, depending on the arena (driven at work, passive at home)?

So many men feel stuck—either paralyzed and unable to move, or unable to stop moving. Which would you say is true of you these days?

ONE FINAL QUESTION

What *would* you have loved to hear from your father? Let's say that your father has died, and you are cleaning out his belongings, going through all his effects. In a desk drawer of his you discover an envelope, with your name on it, written in your father's handwriting. As you think about opening that letter, what would you long for it to say? Is there an apology? An affirmation? Write that letter—not as the one he might have written, but as the one you would have given anything for him to have written. What do you long for it to say from him to you? (Use the previous Field Notes page to write more.)

Take a little bit of time . . . and if your father bestowed a clear sense of masculinity upon you, give great thanks to God for having blessed you with a father who gave to you what so few have had. Ask God to carry you on in your masculine journey, to take you deeper and farther into your heart.

If your father didn't bestow a masculine blessing upon you, take some time right now to lay that before God.

O God, it's true. My heart is wounded within me. Come to me, dear Jesus, speak to my heart such strong and sure words, affirm my masculinity, and grant me the ears to hear you speak those life-giving words. Take me now on the journey of my heart's recovery. Show me more clearly the assault I've endured, and what I've done with my heart over these years. Only keep my heart, I pray, and be my guide every step. In your name I pray.

CHAPTER 5

THE BATTLE FOR A MAN'S HEART

To give a man back his heart is the hardest mission on earth.
FROM THE MOVIE *MICHAEL*

BEFORE SETTING OUT

Two things before you start working through this chapter:

Get together with a few buddies and watch *Gladiator*. What does it stir in your masculine heart?

Begin to take some deliberate steps to care for your masculine heart. I recommend journaling, if you haven't begun already. Capture your thoughts, hang on to what God is opening up in you, write down the questions all this is stirring inside. You might also begin getting together with a few other guys on a fairly regular basis, to share the journey, process life, just adventure together.

GUT REACTION

What's your gut-level reaction to this chapter?

GETTING YOUR BEARINGS

The Goal

The goal of this chapter is to see the emasculation you've endured, to uncover the famished craving you have for validation, and to reveal where you've taken that craving in hopes of an answer. The reason is that we're about to seek the answer God has for us, but it cannot come and we cannot understand his way with us until we see clearly where we've taken our hearts.

Trail Markers

- The assault on a man continues through his life, and its effect is emasculation.
- That assault is far more premeditated than most of us thought.
- The result is a famished craving in the soul—our desperate desire for validation as a man.
- We take our search many places, but eventually we all take it to the Woman, or, in the case of same-sex attraction, to an idealized Man.

SETTING OUT

What was your reaction to my telling Blaine to get up and hit that bully as hard as he possibly can? Are you delighted with it, or appalled? Why? Does your reaction surprise you? Where did it come from? Does your reaction differ from your wife's reaction?

FROM THE MAP

There is a way that appears to be right, but in the end it leads to death.

PROVERBS 14:12

Has anyone done for you what I did for Blaine—intervene at a crucial moment when your soul was hanging in the balance and invite you to be dangerous? And if the answer is no—what is the message of that?

The assault on our masculine heart continues long after our "wound" is given. (And remember, a man is not wounded once, but many times, throughout the course of his life.) Nearly every blow falls in the same place—as an attack on his strength. Life takes it away, one vertebra at a time, until he has no spine left at all. Can you recall other assaults you've endured over the years? To start with, what wounds did you receive at school? Was that a deeply affirming place of your masculine strength? Were you taunted on the playground? Did they have a "name" for you?

What about among your friends? Have they been loyal and affirming?

And at work—are you honored there as a man of strength? Have you ever been stripped of power or position? Are you invited to speak your mind freely? What price have you paid for job security?

How about church—have you been validated as a powerful warrior there? Are you encouraged to buck the system, challenge foolish policies, be yourself? Or is the pressure pretty much to get in line, and don't rock the boat? What happens to people who do rock the boat?

What about in marriage? Does your wife encourage you to be dangerous, to seek adventure, to take risks? Give an example or two.

In what ways does she intentionally arouse you, seduce you with her feminine beauty and affirm you as a man?

And how might she have tried to tame you over the years?

The world is unnerved by a truly masculine man, and so it tries to socialize men away from all that is fierce and wild and passionate. Yet God made men the way they are because we *need* them to be the way they are. As Christina Hoff Sommers said, "The energy, competitiveness, and corporeal daring of normal, decent males is responsible for much of what is right in the world." I cited the safety of a neighborhood, or the bringing down of slavery, or the men who gave their places on the lifeboats of the *Titanic*. Can you name a few more examples of where the nature of men is exactly what the world has *needed*?

I used the example of a scalpel and a stallion, how the *danger* is part of their *goodness*. In the case of the scalpel, you cannot heal unless it is dangerous. In the case of the stallion, you cannot ever have life, foster new life unless you have the danger. What might be different in your world if *you* were far more dangerous? And, who in your life is encouraging you to be that way?

WHAT'S REALLY GOING ON HERE, ANYWAY?

Take a look around you—what do you observe? What do you see in the lives of the men that you work with, live by, go to church alongside? Are they full of passionate freedom? Do they fight well? Are their women deeply grateful for how well their men have loved them? Are their children radiant with affirmation? Think of the men you know, or at least work with or live near. Place their names in one of the following three categories:

They have lost heart, given up, been taken out.

They are wounded men, and though trying they can't seem to get up.

They are among the captives. To what?

I said that this is a battlefield, that we are at war, that in fact we are in the late stages of the long and vicious war against the human heart. Did that sound a bit too dramatic for you? What have you understood the situation to be? Did you write it off to culture, or upbringing, or bad luck?

Have you ever conceived of Life as a *war*?

Had you noticed the deadly accuracy of the wounds you've been given? What have your wounds prevented you from doing in your life? Have you followed your dreams? Are you doing what you wanted to do with your life when you were a young man?

The wounds we've taken were leveled against us with stunning accuracy. Did it occur to you that all those wounds were *aimed*, that they were not random but *intentional*? Does it seem to make a bit more sense now—or do I still sound like a reactionary or a bit overly dramatic?

Hopefully, you're getting the picture. Do you know why there's been such an assault? The Enemy fears you. You are dangerous big-time. If you ever really got your heart back, lived from it with courage, you would be a huge problem to him. You would do a lot of damage . . . on the side of Good. Remember how valiant and effective God has been in the history of the world? You are a stem of that victorious stalk. How does that strike you? What if it *were* true?

Once again, I want to tell you as clearly as I can that you *can* get your heart back. But I also warned you—if you want your heart back, if you want the wound healed and your strength restored and to find your true name, *you're going to have to fight for it*. Notice your reaction to my words. Does not something in you stir a little, a yearning to live? And doesn't another voice rush in, urging caution, maybe wanting to dismiss me altogether? *He's being melodramatic. What arrogance.* Or, *maybe some guys could, but not me.* Or, *I don't know . . . is this really worth it?*

Do you see the Battle in your reaction?

OUR SEARCH FOR AN ANSWER

The bottom line is this: We still need to know what we never heard, or heard so badly, from our fathers. We *need to know* who we are and if we have what it takes. What do we do now with that ultimate question? Where do we go to find an answer? In order to help you find the answer to The Question, let me ask you another: What *have* you done with your question? Where have you taken it? You see, a man's core question does not go away. He may try for years to shove it out of his awareness, and just "get on with life." But it does not go away. It is a hunger so essential to our soul that it will compel us to find a resolution. In truth, it drives everything we do.

Do you see it driving you? In what ways? Peter chose financial success. Brad chose belonging to the group. Where in your life are you looking for the answer to your Question?

 **FIELD NOTES**

DISPATCH

You know, for most of my life the most common adjective you would hear my friends use to describe me was *passionate*. Notice I said "was." In the last four years I have watched my passion shrink. Mostly because I got tired of fighting. It's only a start, but I want to fight again. I want to fight for what makes me come alive. I don't know what this will look like yet, but I know it will look different than my life looks now.

CHRIS

Another way of asking this is, what would it feel like death to lose, or to know you will never, ever attain?

Where does most of the energy of your life get spent in a normal week? And why are you spending it there?

TAKING IT TO EVE

I confessed my long and sad story of searching for "the woman that will make me feel like a man," how I went from girlfriend to girlfriend trying to get an answer to my Question, that I was certain that being the Hero to the Beauty would bring me validation as a man.

What has been your history with women? This is well worth a little more thought here (including for men who experience same-sex attraction, for you, too, have a history with Eve). First, make a list of the names of the key women in your life, the women you've had a relationship with or wanted a relationship with. Start with your first love, your first sweetheart, and go right up to the present, including your wife or current relationship. Then, answer the following questions for each woman:

Who pursued whom? Who initiated the relationship?

What was the relationship like? Was it stormy, placid, passionate, guarded, argumentative, boring?

Who led during the course of the relationship? Who initiated phone calls, chose what you'd do on a date, basically provided the energy behind the relationship? Did that change over time?

How did she make you feel about yourself as a man? What "grade" did she give you, or make you feel (or, what grade did you give yourself because of her)?

Who broke up with whom? How was it done . . . and why? Most important, what was the message to you?

Do you find yourself thinking about her still; does she show up in your dreams?

What were you looking for from her? Do you see the way you took your Question to her?

Now, notice the flow of all your relationships—do you see a pattern emerging?

Do you see how it affected you? Is there a message about you as a man that has taken root?

By the way, this is why so many men secretly fear their wives. A wife sees her husband like no one else does, sleeps with him, knows what he's made of. If he has given her the power to validate him as a man, then he has also given her the power to invalidate him, too. That's the deadly catch. A pastor told me that for years he's been trying to please

DISPATCH

My first girlfriend broke my heart. After that, I played it safe big-time, waiting for a girl to pursue me, never really committing myself or my heart. That went on for years, even into my marriage, I'm sorry to say.

JOHN

his wife, but she keeps giving him an F. "What if she is not the report card on you?" I suggested. "She sure feels like it . . . and I'm failing," he responded.

What grade do you feel you're currently getting from your woman? And what does that make you want to do? (Use the Field Notes page on 122 to record your thoughts.)

THE GOLDEN-HAIRED WOMAN

Why is pornography more addictive for men than heroin? Because that seductive beauty reaches down inside *and touches your desperate hunger for validation as a man you didn't even know you had,* touches it like nothing else most men have ever experienced. You must understand—this is deeper than legs and breasts and good sex. This may be the biggest revelation a man comes to about the Beauty—that his struggle with her is not about sex but about *validation.*

Let me ask you now about the fantasy woman—the woman in your daydreams, the women who make the *Sports Illustrated* swimsuit issue, or perhaps the women you are looking at or talking to on the internet: When you look at her, what does it feel like she is *saying* to *you*?

How does she make you feel *as a man*?

And after the pornographic "affair" is over, how do you feel then? Did it satisfy—meaning, you never need to go back, because you have an Answer to your Question?

We've got to be honest about two things: First, Eve is a garden of delight (Song of Songs 4:16). Man, oh man, is she! Femininity can really arouse masculinity—no question about it. But I'm sorry, Mr. Springsteen, she's *not* everything you want, everything you need—not even close. Of course it will stay "a million miles away."

You can't get there from here because it's not there. It's not there. The answer to your Question can never, ever be found there. Has that ever really sunk in to you? Let it now. Put your pen down and just sit with this thought for a few minutes: *I will never find what I'm looking for in a woman.* What happens in your heart as you allow that to be true? Is it sadness? Emptiness? Relief?

DISPATCH

I confessed in a previous book the major revelation I came to one day about the Beauty. Because it bears on this issue so directly, permit me to repeat it here:

> I was walking down the hall at work one day, lost in my thoughts. Walking ahead of me, the same direction I was going, was a beautiful woman. I looked up and my heart said *Wow.* Fearing that the beast of lust was rearing its ugly head, I tried to kill my reaction. It never works, and I knew it, so I decided instead to find out what was going on beneath what seemed to be an inappropriate response. Still walking along, with this beauty still in view, I asked my heart, *what do you mean by "wow"?* The next sentence literally popped out, unscripted, from some place deep inside me. *The grand prize if you are truly a man.* I was stunned. I have lived that lie for a long time. How many young boys in our culture, just as they are entering adolescence, are introduced to sexuality as masculinity? Look at every ad designed for men. Whether it's for cars or sporting gear, clothes or beer, there is almost always a beautiful siren posing seductively alongside. The message is beaten into us—if you're a man, you'll win the woman. I saw how long I had been haunted by that idea, and I also saw that what I was desiring was not an affair, but a truer sense of my own masculinity.

THE JOURNEY OF DESIRE

A BREAK IN THE CLOUDS

This subject is far too important to give only a paragraph, but I knew I couldn't offer what was needed here. It wants a book in itself, though I do hope *Wild at Heart* will be helpful to men struggling with homosexual feelings. So let me recommend two books: Nicolosi's book: *Reparative Therapy of Male Homosexuality*, which is a bit clinical but very good, and I also want to recommend Leanne Payne's book *A Crisis in Masculinity*, because the stories she tells there of the healing of men's souls is so hopeful for gay men.

ON HOMOSEXUALITY

Or is there a fantasy man? I wrote in the book that homosexual men are actually more clear on this point—that they know what is missing in their hearts is masculine love. The problem is that they've sexualized it. Joseph Nicolosi says that homosexuality is an attempt to repair the wound by filling it with masculinity, either the masculine love that was missing or the masculine strength many men feel they do not possess. It, too, is a vain search, and that is why the overwhelming number of homosexual relationships do not last, why so many gay men move from one man to another and why so many of them suffer from depression and a host of other addictions. What they need can't be found there.

Why have I said all this about our search for validation and the answer to our Question? Because we cannot hear the real answer until we see we've got a false one. As long as we chase the illusion, how can we face reality? The hunger is there; it lives in our souls like a famished craving, no matter what we've tried to fill it with. If you take your question to Eve, it will break your heart. I know this now, after many, many hard years. You can't get your answer there. In fact, you can't get your answer from any of the things men chase after to find their sense of self. There is only one source for the answer to your Question. And so no matter where you've taken your Question, you've got to take it back. You have to walk away.

Will you? How . . . and when? What will you give up in order to find the Real Thing?

> *Father, I want to know You, but my coward heart fears to give up its toys. I cannot part with them without inward bleeding, and I do not try to hide from You the terror of the parting. I come trembling, but I do come. Please root from my heart all those things which I have cherished so long and which have become a very part of my living self, so that You may enter and dwell there without a rival. In Jesus' Name, Amen. (A.W. Tozer, The Pursuit of God)*

CHAPTER 6

THE FATHER'S VOICE

Who can give a man this, his own name?
GEORGE MACDONALD

BEFORE SETTING OUT

Again, I'm going to urge you to do two things before you start working through this chapter:

Watch *Groundhog Day*. The character played by Bill Murray is a poser extraordinaire. His life begins to change when God pins him down over and over again until he finally gives up his plan for making his life work, including his attempt to get the Woman to validate him.

Second, ask your wife to read through *Wild at Heart* on her own. I know—it's going to raise a lot of questions and expectations on her part, but this is so revolutionary that she's got to know what you are doing and why.

GUT REACTION

What are you really struck by? What did it make you want to do?

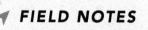 **FIELD NOTES**

GETTING YOUR BEARINGS

The Goal

You have an opportunity now to completely reframe your relationship with God, where he becomes the one who is initiating you, taking you on the masculine journey. Actually, he has been trying to do that for some time now. You can choose to give up the false self and walk away from the Woman as the one who validates you—or God can bring it all down. The choice is yours.

Trail Markers

- The history of a man's relationship with God is the story of how God calls him out, takes him on a journey, and gives him his true name.
- God's initiation of a man must take a very cunning course; he will wound us in the very place where we have been wounded.
- If we would walk with him in our initiatory journey, we must walk away from the false self—set it down, give it up willingly.
- Because so many of us turned to the Woman for our sense of masculinity, we must "walk away" from her as well—only in the sense that you stop asking her to validate you as a man.

SETTING OUT

The theme of the chapter is *initiation*—that mysterious and now lost process whereby a boy becomes a man *and knows it*. We need initiation, but the way in which God initiates us often comes in a surprising direction: thwarting our false self, our plan for redemption, and taking us into our wound. Most of us have been misinterpreting what God is doing in our lives for a long time.

Recall the story I tell about the day on the ranch when Pop sent me to get the steer—alone. Did that stir anything in you? Do you have a story like it, maybe not from a ranch of course, but a day in your life when you were called

FIELD NOTES

out like that by someone who believed in you—when you felt both a little scared and also honored, *believed* in? What happened?

I said that I got the steer that day . . . and a whole lot more. What do you think I got? What did *you* get on your day?

I hope that by now you've seen the scene I describe from *Gladiator* (and I strongly urge you to). Tell me what it awakens in you. Does it stir you in any way? Could you answer like that? Do you long to?

FIELD NOTES

A BREAK IN THE CLOUDS

COMMODUS: Your fame is well deserved, Spaniard. I don't believe there's ever been a gladiator that matched you . . . Why doesn't the hero reveal himself and tell us all your real name? (*Maximus is silent.*) You do have a name?

MAXIMUS: My name is Gladiator. (*He turns and walks away.*)

COMMODUS: How dare you show your back to me?! Slave! You will remove your helmet and tell me your name.

MAXIMUS: (*Slowly, very slowly, lifts his helmet and turns to face his enemy*): My name is Maximus Decimus Meridius; commander of the Armies of the North; general of the Felix Legions; loyal servant to the true emperor, Marcus Aurelius; father to a murdered son; husband to a murdered wife and I will have my vengeance, in this life or in the next.

His answer builds like a mighty wave, swelling in size and strength before it crashes on the shore.

We *desperately* need to know our name, the way Maximus knew his. So much else hangs on this—our sense of mission, or purpose in life, our ability to fight for others, and especially our impact on those we love most. But as I warned, I don't mean know in the way we "know" about the Battle of Waterloo or the ozone layer. I mean know in the deep, personal, firsthand experience way. Adam didn't know facts *about* Eve (Eve is a hominid as I am; a female of my species; she has brown hair and green eyes; she is not a horse or a moth). He knew Eve deeply, intimately (very intimately). Over the course of your Christian life, how would you classify your knowledge of God . . . and of yourself?

A BREAK IN THE CLOUDS

When I talk about knowing our "true name," I hope you understand that I mean it in a metaphorical, or symbolical, way. Jacob was given his first name at birth, for he came out of the womb "grasping" Esau's heel. (Jacob means "supplanter," "trickster," or "he deceives.") For many years he lived out the identity that went along with that name—getting his brother to sell him his birthright for a bowl of porridge, tricking his father into giving him the blessing, living off his cleverness, grasping. But there came a time in Jacob's life when God changed his name—when through a great trial he both crippled him and blessed him. God gave him the new name Israel—which means "he who wrestles with God." (A much more noble identity, wouldn't you say?)

The name given us in life—whether our actual name or a nickname or just the deep identity bestowed on us—is often far from who *we truly are* in God's eyes, the man he created us to be. So to speak of finding our true name is to describe that process whereby we shed the old identity for a new one; with that new identity comes a deeper strength, a life mission, a sense of self given to us by God. And yes, it may be embodied in an actual name like Israel, or it may be contained in a series of new "names" or phrases such as "one who fights for the truth" or "tender warrior."

Most of us have been misinterpreting life and what God is doing for a long time. "I think I'm just trying to get God to make my life work easier," a client of mine confessed, but he could have been speaking for most of us. We're asking the wrong questions. Most of us are asking, "God, why did you let this happen to me?" Or, "God, why won't you just . . ." (fill in the blank—help me succeed, get my kids to straighten out, fix my marriage—you know what you've been whining about). And before reading this chapter, what would you say God has been up to in your life over these past few years—I mean, how would you describe his activity or nonactivity in your life? What has God been up to with you?

And what are the questions you've been asking God? What has been the subject of your prayers, that is, before reading *Wild at Heart*?

INITIATION

Where can you go to learn an answer like the one Maximus was able to give—to learn your true name, a name that can never be taken from you? That deep heart knowledge comes only through a process of *initiation*.

The history of a man's relationship with God is the story of how God calls him out, takes him on a journey, and gives him his true name. Most of us have thought it was the story of how God sits on his throne waiting to whack a man broadside when he steps out of line. Not so. He created Adam for adventure, battle, and beauty; He created us for a unique place in his story, and he is committed to bringing us back to the original design. So God calls Abram out from Ur of the Chaldeans to a land he has never seen, to the frontier, and along the way Abram gets a new name. He becomes Abraham. God takes Jacob off into Mesopotamia somewhere, to learn things he has to learn and cannot learn at his mother's side. When he rides back into town, he has a limp and a new name as well.

Even if your father did his job, he can only take you part of the way. There comes a time when you have to leave all that is familiar and go on into the unknown with God.

Now let this question be from God to you: *Will you let me initiate you?*

A BREAK IN THE CLOUDS

There's a new interest in "initiation" these days, and a number of books are beginning to surface on how to take a boy into manhood. Most of it seems to focus on various rites of passage—Christian "bar mitzvahs" and such. And while it can be very powerful to tell a boy that he is now a man, and speak into his life words of affirmation and counsel, that cannot take the place of *experiences* through which the boy discovers the truth for himself, where he moves into *knowledge* of his strength and name. That's the first point I want to clarify—that initiation requires *a guided process of personal discovery.* As I wrote, "You have to know where you've come from; you have to have faced a series of trials that test you; you have to have taken a journey; and you have to have faced your enemy." *That* is the process of initiation, or at least, the broad outlines of it.

Second, what is to be discovered by this boy (or this man, who, though fifty-two, still needs to know these things)? That he is a good boy, and knows his memory verses, or *that he is a dangerous man with a dangerous mission and he has what it takes to fulfill it?* The process all depends on the revelation and the training that are to be imparted, which in God's case is far more dangerous than most Christian camp experiences imply. It could cost you your life.

Finally, in nearly every case, *the process is mostly a mystery to the initiate.* His elders know what they are doing, but the young man does not know what's coming next. Why this trial, and not another one? Why this long? As he goes on, some of that mystery begins to be replaced with the wisdom of experience: *Oh, I recognize some of this—I've faced something like this before, and I remember what to do.* The mystery gives way to wisdom, BUT NEVER TO FORMULA, for no two situations are ever identical, and no two men are ever alike.

To enter into a journey of initiation with God requires a new set of questions: What are you trying to teach me here? What issues in my heart are you trying to raise through this? What is it you want me to see? What are you asking me to let go of? Looking at our relationship with God in this way provides us with an entirely new orientation: God is initiating me. That gives us a whole new way of interpreting events, a new set of questions to be asking. How different would the past five years have been for you if you had seen them as a process of initiation, and asked those questions as all the things that have unfolded took place?

HOW YOU'VE HANDLED YOUR WOUND

Actually, God has been trying to initiate you for a long time. What is in the way is how you've mishandled your wound and the life you've constructed as a result. Most men *minimize* their wound. They either . . .

1. Deny it outright ("naw, nothing like that ever really happened to me" or "I had a pretty good life"), or they
2. Leave it in the past ("that was a long time ago and I've gotten over it" or "I can't remember much from my youth"), or they
3. Minimize the impact of the wound ("It just didn't really matter that much to me" or "Lots of tough things happen to people . . . so?"). Other men may admit the wound but mishandle it because they *embrace* it or its message . . .
4. "Yes, it was awful, but I deserved it," or
5. "But what he said was true about me," or
6. They take on a victim mentality and let the wound define them, embracing it to the point of needing the wound ("I'm weak . . . take care of me. And don't ever require me to be a man").

How have you handled your wound? And why did you choose that answer? Give a few examples.

WARNING!

God is committed to you, but some of you might be feeling that this just isn't going to be true for you—that sure, God probably does take some men on a special journey, but not you. Whose voice do you suppose is speaking? Is it consistent with God's word to you, promises like "I will guide you along the best pathway for your life. I will advise you and watch over you" (Psalm 32:8 NLT)?

Most men deny their wound—deny that it happened, deny that it hurt, certainly deny that it's shaping the way they live today. And so God's initiation of a man must take a very cunning course; a course that feels really odd, even cruel. He will wound us in the very place where we have already been wounded.

THWARTING THE FALSE SELF

Okay, so now we have a new orientation—that God is initiating us, taking us on a mysterious and dangerous journey that will reveal to us our true name and our real place in his story. We also know that he does it in a most surprising—and disruptive—way, by thwarting the false self and even wounding us in the place of our deepest wound. We also have a new set of questions to be asking, not "Why did you allow this to happen?" but rather, "What issues in my heart are you trying to raise through this?"

Without doing any further excavation, do you have a pretty good hunch where God has been thwarting *you*? Why did you choose that?

Let's do a little excavation. Be straightforward now: What's basically been your plan for making life work? And what was the "golden bat" you brought to that plan?

Example: *Life will work out if I'm successful,* and I chose that route because I'm good at making money but not good at much else. Or, *life will work out if I'm liked by everyone,* and I chose that route because I can be such a good guy, and all my

DISPATCH

I am forty-eight years old. Today I am several weeks away from completing a legal separation from my second wife at her request. I have not been the man God intended, and all this is causing me to examine myself. I am afraid of what I will discover. I pray I am courageous enough to follow through and once again become "wild at heart."

JESS

life I've been the one everybody liked. Or, *life will work out so long as I don't get close to anyone,* and I chose that route because I'm an intellectually oriented guy who is uncomfortable with intimacy.

How's it going? Is your plan working?

Where isn't your life going well right now? Where are you experiencing the most disappointment or "frustration" in your life? What are you thinking about when you awaken at 2:00 A.M.?

Your career—how are things going there? Are you in your dream job—and is it flowing without interruption?

DISPATCH

I remember overhearing a man I admire talking candidly about his plan for life. He said, "I'm basically trying to make all the money I can and get as far ahead as possible before the bottom drops out . . . because I know one day it will." He was a Christian counselor, by the way, and his plan struck me as a curious way to serve God.

Your marriage (or pursuit of the Woman)—is it all you dreamed it would be?

And, if you have children, is everything terrific on that front?

Where in your life are you feeling vulnerable, or exposed, perhaps on shaky ground? Are you being asked to step into an arena you really fear? Are you being asked to let go of something that's meant the world to you?

And, looking over the previous seven questions, what are you doing in response to those areas that aren't going that great—maybe even going miserably? Are you scrambling to make it right? Where is most of the energy in your life going right now . . . and why are you investing it there? What are you hoping to remedy?

A BREAK IN THE CLOUDS

Try it—give up all your comforters for one week, even the ones that don't seem illicit or any sort of problem. Just let yourself go without them and notice what they've been keeping at bay— notice what emotions surface without them. Then ask yourself, *Why am I feeling that? Where is this coming from?*

Where are you losing passion . . . maybe giving up, going into resignation? Why?

Have you noticed any of your addictions flaring up over the past year? Is there a new struggle now that wasn't a struggle before? Might you be numbing some of your pain with an anesthetic (like working late, eating too much, watching TV, checking out through a hobby, masturbating)?

And if *relief* could come, if something could happen in your life that would make you much happier, what would that be?

Could it be that God is thwarting some aspect of your false self, thwarting some part of your plan for making life work? Why would he be closing in on that?

FIELD NOTES

DISPATCH

My deep father-wound came in part from my dad's alcoholism, his addiction. I turned to the Woman to give me what my father did not give, turned to Eve's daughters in place of my God. So God in turn gave me my worst nightmare: a woman with an addiction. He did it out of a "severe mercy" (to borrow VanAuken's terribly beautiful phrase), a wound to bring me to face my other wound, and at the same time bring down the idol I had given my heart away to.

JOHN

In order to take a man into his wound, so that he can heal it and begin the release of the true self, God will thwart the false self. He will take away all that you've leaned upon to bring you life. What's your reaction to reading that? What do you fear God will take away?

But does this idea of God thwarting to save you help you to understand a struggle or trial in your life? What does it help you reinterpret in the past several years?

Every man has a plan for salvation, for making his life work. (Some of you are well on your way of repenting of that, and I'm cheering.) The plan is formed as a defense against the wound, against further exposure, and as an attempt to get some taste of what he was made for but in a way that's well within his control. That's why I said, "The real journey begins when the false self fails . . . If we would walk with him in our journey of masculine initiation, we must walk away from the false self—set it down, give it up willingly . . . We can choose to do it ourselves, or we can wait for God to bring it all down." So—what do you need to give up, walk away from, set down? What would feel really risky to do, really naked, really require faith right now?

WALKING AWAY FROM THE WOMAN

As we walk away from the false self, we will feel vulnerable and exposed. We will be sorely tempted to turn to our comforters for some relief, those places that we've found solace and rest. Because so many of us turned to the Woman for our sense of masculinity, we must walk away from her as well. *I do not mean you leave your wife.* I mean you stop looking to her to validate you, stop trying to make her come through for you, stop trying to get your answer from her. For some men, this may mean disappointing her. If you've been a passive man, tip-toeing around your wife for years, never doing anything to rock the boat, then it's time to rock it. Stand up to her; get her mad at you. For those of you violent men (including achievers), it means *you stop abusing her.* You release her as the object of your anger because you release her as the one who was supposed to make you a man. Repentance for a driven man means you become *kind.* Both types—passive and violent men—are still going to the Woman. Repentance depends on which way you've approached her.

How have you handled the Woman in your life? Have you been more passive and fearful, or more "violent" and angry? Why? For how long?

What *have* you been seeking from your woman?

What does it mean for *you* to "walk away from the woman"?

WARNING!

This is a very dangerous moment, when God seems set against everything that has meant life to us. Satan spies his opportunity, and leaps to accuse God in our hearts. You see, he says, *God is angry with you. He's disappointed in you. If he loved you, he would make things smoother. He's not out for your best, you know.* The Enemy always tempts us back toward control, to recover and rebuild the false self. We must remember that it is out of love that God thwarts our impostor. As Hebrews reminds us, it is the son whom God disciplines, therefore do not lose heart (12:5–6).

⁜ *FIELD NOTES*

WARNING!

This is not an excuse to get out of a tough relationship nor is it permission to divorce or abandon in any way. The point is this: Most men turn at some point to the woman for their validation as a man. This is nearly universal. So to recover their masculine journey, they need to stop doing that. It's not so much that we walk away from the woman as it is that we walk *toward* God, toward a bigger orbit, so that we might learn to love her instead of seeking our validation from her.

A man needs a much bigger orbit than a woman. He needs a mission, a life purpose, and he needs to know his name. Only then is he fit for a woman, for only then does he have something to invite her into. What's your mission? What are you inviting your woman to join you in?

Ask your woman this question: "What could I do—or stop doing—that would feel like a great relief to you in our relationship?"

We only "walk away" from the Woman because we have some "soul work to do." As Bly wrote,

> What does it mean when a man falls in love with a radiant face across the room? It may mean that he has some soul work to do. His soul is the issue. Instead of pursuing the woman and trying to get her alone . . . he needs to go alone himself, perhaps to a mountain cabin for three months, write poetry, canoe down a river, and dream. That would save some women a lot of trouble.

What is the soul work you have to do? Can you get some time away?

WARNING!

Wild at Heart is so potentially revolutionary that it would be a very good idea to have your wife read it on her own so that she can understand what's going on with you!

The bottom line is this: We must reverse Adam's choice; we must choose God over Eve. We must take our ache to him, for only in God will we find the healing of our wound.

O God, I have tasted Your goodness, and it has both satisfied me and made me thirsty for more. I am painfully conscious of my need of further grace. I am ashamed of my lack of desire. O God, the Triune God, I want to want You; I long to be filled with longing; I thirst to be made more thirsty still. Show me Your glory, I pray You, that so I may know You indeed. Begin in mercy a new work of love within me. Say to my soul, "Rise up, my love, my fair one, and come away." Then give me grace to rise and follow You up from this misty lowland where I have wandered so long. In Jesus' Name, Amen. (A.W. Tozer, The Pursuit of God)

CHAPTER 7

HEALING THE WOUND

The deepest desire of our hearts is for union with God. God created us
for union with Himself: This is the original purpose of our lives.

BRENNAN MANNING

BEFORE SETTING OUT

Three things before you start working through this chapter:

Reread the chapter in the book.

Go back into chapter 4 in this guide and review your work there, what you
remembered and discovered about your wound. That needs to be fresh in your
mind and heart for this chapter's work.

Watch *Good Will Hunting*, with special focus on Will's wound, how he's handled it, and the healing that takes place through his relationship with Sean and
with his "brothers," the male friends Will has. My only real warnings about the
film are the rough language, and the way it tries to make the conclusion about
the woman—but chapter 10 will sort that out.

GUT REACTION

As always, I think it's best to start with a gut reaction to the chapter. What are you really struck by? What did this chapter make you want to do?

GETTING YOUR BEARINGS

The Goal

Our goal here is the healing of your wound, and the discovering of your true name. It's the most important work in all the book, for every chapter we've done thus far has led up to this, and every chapter that follows relies upon the work of God here.

Trail Markers

- It's not a sign of weakness that you need God desperately—you were meant to live in a deeply dependent relationship with him.
- The healing of your wound begins by no longer despising those broken places within you. We offer compassion to our broken places.
- You'll find the healing of your masculine soul through a process that by its nature has to be very personal—yet there are several phases I lay out below.
- God has a new name for us, and hearing that name is a deep part of the healing process. That name reveals our true strength, our glory, and our calling.

THOSE BROKEN PLACES WITHIN US

Most men, including myself, are embarrassed by their emptiness and woundedness. We feel ashamed that we are not stronger, more together, farther down the road. We know we are meant to embody strength, we know we are not what we

FIELD NOTES

FROM THE MAP

. . . help me for your name's sake;
    out of the goodness of your love,
    deliver me.
For I am poor and needy,
    and my heart is wounded within me . . .
Help me, LORD my God;
    save me according to your
    unfailing love.

PSALM 109:21–22, 26

were meant to be, and so we feel our brokenness as a source of shame. As we spoke of his wound recently, and how he needed to enter into it for healing, Dave protested. "I don't even want to go there. It all feels so true." How are you feeling about entering into your wound?

Many men report feeling as though there is a boy inside, that something within them feels small and weak and fearful. As I said, the road to my healing began when I realized that something in me felt young—like a ten-year-old boy in a man's world but without a man's ability to come through. There was so much fear beneath the surface: fear that I would fail, fear that I would be found out, and finally, fear that I was ultimately on my own. *Where did all this fear come from?* I wondered. *Why do I feel so alone in the world . . . and so young inside? Why does something in my heart feel orphaned?* Have you felt something like that within you? Are you aware of your wound, and those young and orphaned places?

Sadly, most of us despise that about ourselves, and we're harsh with the broken places within us. *Quit being such a baby,* we order ourselves inside. So much of my drivenness over the years came as a way of forcing those places to "get with the program," buck up, stop crying, and act like a man. How have you treated your wounded heart, your brokenness?

Jesus said, "It would be better to be thrown into the sea with a large millstone tied around the neck than to face the punishment in store for harming one of these little ones" (Luke 17:2 NLT). God is *furious* about what's happened to you—he's not angry with you, he's angry *for* you. Turn the tables for a moment and think of how you would feel if the wounds you were given, the blows dealt to you, were dealt to a boy you loved—your son, perhaps. Would you shame him for it? Would you feel scorn that he couldn't rise above it all? What would you want for him?

The scene from *Good Will Hunting*, where Sean says over and over again to Will that what he went through as a boy was not his fault—how did that scene strike you? Put yourself in Will's place for a moment, and let it be true for you. All that happened—your father's wounding of you, the way the world emasculated you—none of that was your fault. Don't reason back and forth; you might not even think that it *was* your fault. Don't try to "feel" anything. Just stay with the sentence for awhile, allow that to be true for you. *It's not your fault.* What rises in your heart?

How do you feel about needing help? Have you ever asked for help with your wound, your brokenness? Most of us are fiercely independent; we never even stop to ask for directions, let alone for something as deep as help with our own soul. But what if it were okay, simply the way we're all made? What if receiving help was normal for a man, and meant nothing about failure or weakness?

A BREAK IN THE CLOUDS

Desperado, why don't you come to your senses
You've been out riding fences for so long now
Oh you're a hard one, but I know that you got your reasons
These things that are pleasin' you will hurt you somehow

Desperado, you know you ain't getting younger
Your pain and your hunger are drivin' you home
And freedom, O freedom, well that's just some people talkin'
Your prison is walkin' through this world all alone

Desperado, why don't you come to your senses
Come down from your fences, open the gate
It may be rainin', but there's a rainbow above you
You'd better let somebody love you
Before it's too late

THE EAGLES "DESPERADO"
by Glenn Fry and Don Henley (1973)

ENTERING THE WOUND—
THE DOORWAYS

Buechner was so right when he said that we bury our wound deep, and after a while we never take it out again, let alone speak of it. But take it out we must—or better, enter into it. The reason is that we cannot be healed from ten miles away; Christ must *touch us*, and touch us *where we hurt most*.

There are many doorways God can use to take us back into our wound . . .

You'll remember Brad's story, how he longed to belong to the group? God took him into his wound by taking the group away. Dave sought his "healing" through the Woman; God took the Woman away. What has God taken away from you that has felt earthshaking? What has he thwarted, to get you into your wound?

I also confessed that it was my anger that caused me to stop and look under the hood. That might be another door God uses—if you've been feeling angry or "frustrated" lately, go back to that. Ask yourself, *What's underneath the anger? Why am I so mad?*

Another route may be your addictions, for they are what you use to numb your pain. What if you let each one go? What if you never, ever had it again—what does that bring up in your heart? Is it fear, or sadness? What's beneath *that*?

God used several movies with me, among them *A River Runs Through It* and *A Perfect World*. Has a film or a song or a story brought you to tears, maybe for reasons you couldn't explain? It would be good to go back to that again, to use it as a doorway for this journey.

Above all else, we offer a simple prayer:

Jesus, take me into my wound. I give you permission and access to my soul and to my deepest hurts. Come, and bring me to my own brokenness. Come and shepherd the orphaned boy within me. Let me be fully present to my wounded heart. Uncover my wound and meet me there.

THE WAY OF HEALING

The way in which God heals our wound is a deeply personal process. For one man it happens in a dramatic moment; for another, it takes place over time. Even after we've experienced some real healing, God will often take us back again, a year or two later, for a deeper work of healing. And so what I offer here is not a formula, but a way toward healing—a way that has helped me and many other men.

SURRENDER

It all begins with surrender—that act of the will whereby we give ourselves back to God. As C. S. Lewis said, "Until you have given yourself to him you will not have a real self." So many of us have lived independently for so long—even men who call themselves Christians. Their faith has been more about practicing principles and maintaining morality than it has been about deep communion with God. May I recommend a prayer like this:

Dear Jesus, I am yours. You have ransomed me with your own life, bought me with your own blood. Forgive me for all my years of independence—all my striving, all my retreating, all my self-centeredness and self-determination. I give myself back to you—all of me. I give my body to you as a living sacrifice. I give my soul to you as well—my desperate search for life and love and validation, all my self-protecting, all those parts in me I like and all those I do not like. I give to you my spirit also, to be restored in union with you, for as the Scripture says, "He who unites himself with the Lord is one spirit with him." Forgive me, cleanse me, take me and make me utterly yours. In your name I pray.

RENOUNCE THE VOW

You'll remember that back in chapter 4 I described the vow many of us make after we are wounded—a vow that in some way protects us from ever being hurt again. The only thing more tragic than the tragedy that happens to us is the way we handle it—the choices we make, the person we become, the life we live (or don't live). Jesus said, "Whoever seeks to save his life will lose it" (Luke 17:33 NKJV). The things we do to protect and preserve our hearts usually end up hurting us more. To choose to shut your heart to love—so that you won't be hurt—is to deny the very thing you are made for. To demand perfection of yourself so that no one will ever criticize you again is to lay an intolerable burden on your own back. As Buechner said,

> To do for yourself the best that you have it in you to do—to grit your teeth and clench your fists in order to survive the world at its harshest and worst—is, by that very act, to be unable to let something be done for you and in you that is more wonderful still. The trouble with steeling yourself against the harshness of reality is that the same steel that secures your life against being destroyed secures your life also against being opened up and transformed. (*The Sacred Journey*)

You must renounce that vow deliberately, and out loud. The vow is a kind of agreement with the lie. For example, the lie might have been "You are on your own" and the vow says "Okay—I will never trust anyone again, never let them close." That sort of agreement gives a kind of permission to our Enemy to set up shop there; it acts as a kind of covenant with independence, and therefore sin, and therefore Satan. Do you see how dangerous that is?

Breaking the vow is your way of canceling all agreements with the lie and taking back any ground you gave to the Enemy. It releases your soul for Christ to come in. This is something you must do, for Christ will not violate your will. You made the vow; you must renounce it.

Jesus, I renounce every vow I've made to seal off my wound and protect myself from further pain. Reveal to me what those vows were. [If you can name them specifically, do so, and renounce them.] I break every agreement I have made with

FIELD NOTES

WARNING!

Agnes Sanford was right when she said, "There are in many of us wounds so deep that only the mediation of someone else to whom we may 'bare our grief' can heal us." I had the help of my dear friend Brent, who was also a counselor. You may want to bring this process to a man (preferably) or a woman who is known for his or her wisdom in the healing of the soul. (Sadly, that excludes many church leaders because they just don't know the way of healing.) Having someone walk with you through the restoration of your heart is something I strongly encourage.

the lies that came with my wounds, the lies of Satan, and I make all agreement with you, Jesus. I give the protection of my heart and soul back to you, trust you with all that is within me. In your name I pray.

INVITATION

And then we invite Jesus into our wound, ask him to come and meet us there, to enter into the broken and unhealed places of our hearts and make us whole. All our healing and all our strength flows from our union with Christ. If we would be a "stem of that victorious stock," then we must return every part of this branch we call ourselves to him who is our trunk. It might help to pray the very promise Jesus gave to us when he announced his mission and purpose as our Messiah:

> The Spirit of the Sovereign LORD is on me,
>   because the LORD has anointed me
>   to preach good news to the poor.
> He has sent me to bind up the brokenhearted,
>   to proclaim freedom for the captives
>   and release from darkness for the prisoners,
> to proclaim the year of the LORD's favor
>   and the day of vengeance of our God,
> to comfort all who mourn,
>   and provide for those who grieve in Zion—
> to bestow on them a crown of beauty
>   instead of ashes,
> the oil of joy
>   instead of mourning,
> and a garment of praise
>   instead of a spirit of despair.
>
> Isaiah 61:1–3

And precious Jesus, I invite you into the wounded places of my heart, give you permission to enter every broken place, every young and orphaned part of me. Come, dear Lord, and meet me there. Bind up my heart as you promised to do; heal me and make my heart whole and healthy. Release my heart from every form of captivity and from every form of bondage. Restore and set free my heart, my soul, my mind, and my strength. Help me to mourn, and comfort me as I do. Grant my soul that noble crown of strength instead of ashes; anoint me with the oil of gladness in every grieving part; grant me a garment of praise in place of a spirit of despair. O come to me, Jesus, and surround me with your healing presence. Restore me through union with you. I ask in your name.

WE GRIEVE

Oh how important this step is, for so many of us have never allowed our heart to express its pain and loss, to shed the tears that our wound *deserves*. What a milestone day it was for me when I simply allowed myself to say that the loss of my father *mattered*. The tears that flowed were the first I'd ever granted my wound, and they were deeply healing. All those years of sucking it up melted away in my grief.

It is so important for us to grieve our wound; it is the only honest thing to do. For in grieving we admit the truth—that we were hurt by someone we loved, that we lost something very dear, and it hurt us very much. Tears are healing. They help to open and cleanse the wound. As Augustine wrote in his *Confessions*, "The tears . . . streamed down, and I let them flow as freely as they would, making of them a pillow for my heart. On them it rested." Grief is a form of validation; it says the wound *mattered*.

Yes, Jesus—I confess that it mattered. It mattered deeply. Come into my soul and release the grief and tears bottled up within me. Help me to grieve my own wounds and sorrows.

Grief often has to sneak up on us, because we are so reluctant to allow it expression. Simply let it show up when it chooses to. In the days ahead, allow the tears to come out when they do begin to come. Don't push them down.

WE LET GOD LOVE US

Most men bury their longing to be loved somewhere back in their story. We do it because we were hurt, and we do it because needing love feels weak and "unmanly."

Yes, to be loved is to be hurt. That's why loving and being loved is a sign of great *courage and strength*. After all, Jesus loved us right up to the point of his own death.

As John said at the Last Supper, "Having loved his own who were in the world, he loved them to the end" (John 13:1). The most manly of us all was the most loving.

And as for needing love, again we find in Jesus something really surprising. What he most deeply craves, what he talks about with deepest delight is the Father's love and delight in him. This isn't a source of embarrassment to Christ; quite the opposite. He brags about his relationship with his Father. He's happy to tell anyone who will listen, "The Father and I are one" (John 10:30 NLT). They are *intimate*; they delight in each other.

Abiding in the love of God is our only hope, the only true home for our hearts. It's not that we mentally acknowledge that God loves us. It's that we let our hearts come home to him, and stay in his love. How? How does anyone love and let himself be loved? There is no formula to that, but here are a few thoughts . . .

It begins by not turning to our "other lovers," all those things we've used to comfort our hearts and make us feel validated and numb our pain. Let them go—even legitimate things like the gym or good food. For how long? Longer than you're comfortable with, long enough to let your heart's longing to be loved come to the surface.

And we choose to open our heart to God, to make ourselves vulnerable to him. It might help to pray about what Paul felt was so needed that he included it in his letter to the Ephesians (see 3:16–20):

> *Father, strengthen me with your true strength, by your Spirit in my innermost being, so that Jesus may live intimately in my heart. O let me be rooted and grounded in love, so that I, too, with all your precious saints, may know the fullness of the love of Jesus for me—its height and depth, its length and breadth. Let me be filled with real knowing of your love—even though I will never fully reason it or comprehend it—so that I might be filled with all the life and power you have for me. Do this in me, beyond all that I am able to ask or imagine.*

And then we *allow it to be true* that he does love us—we hold that truth in our hearts before we feel anything. God has loved you with an everlasting love. Before you were ever born he had his eye on you, chose you to be his son. And he proved it beyond all doubt by sending Jesus to the cross for you. (Jeremiah 31:3; Ephesians 1:4–5; Romans 5:8).

FIELD NOTES

WARNING!

Do you bring this up with him? Is this act of forgiveness something you do face-to-face? Only if he has asked to talk about it. God stands ready to forgive us, but we must come to him and ask forgiveness, repent of our wrongdoing. So, too, Jesus warns us not to cast our pearls before swine (Matthew 7:6). He isn't saying your dad is a pig, but rather don't offer forgiveness to someone who couldn't begin to understand how precious it is, someone who would just trample it in the mud. This is between you and God, for the time being.

Finally, we *stay* with that truth for more than thirty seconds. We let it linger in our heart and mind throughout the days ahead—no matter what else occurs to us, or happens around us.

FORGIVENESS

The time has come for us to forgive our fathers. For what? You know better than I. For the wound—or wounds. For the ways he failed you. For things he did and said *and* for things he did *not* do and did *not* say. Forgiveness is far more real and meaningful when we are specific about what we are forgiving. A quick, sweeping "Okay . . . I forgive my dad" is not going to be helpful.

First, write down the things your father did or said, or did not do or say that have hurt you, especially as a boy. Your list doesn't need to be pages in length, but it does need to include the major blows.

Now, as I said, this is an act of the will—not a feeling. We choose to forgive our father whether or not we feel forgiving toward him. Quite often the feelings come sometime later. And remember—forgiving is not saying, *It didn't really matter*; it is not saying, *I probably deserved part of it anyway.* Forgiveness says, *It was wrong, it mattered, and I release you.*

> *Jesus, I choose to forgive my father for all the pain and all the wounds he gave to me. [It will help to be very specific here—to name those wounds and events.] It was wrong, it hurt me deeply, and I choose now to pardon him, because your sacrifice on the cross was enough to pay for these sins. I release my father to you. I also release any bitterness I've harbored toward him, and I ask you to come and cleanse these wounds and heal them. In your name I pray.*

OUR NEW NAME

Then we ask God to be our father, and to tell us our true name. You must ask God what he thinks of you, what he sees in you, and you must stay with the question until you get an answer.

> *Father, who am I to you? You are my true Father—my Creator, my Redeemer, and my Sustainer. You know the man you had in mind when you made me. You know*

*my true name. O Father, I ask you to speak to me, to reveal to me my true strength
and my real name. Open my eyes that I might see, give me ears to hear your voice.
Father, I ask that you speak it not once, but again and again so that I might really
receive it. And grant me the courage to receive what you say and the faith to believe
it. In Jesus' name.*

ON HEARING GOD'S VOICE

God "speaks" to us in many ways. First, there is his written word—the Bible. He
spoke to us in black and white because we needed something rock-solid to build
on. Every other "revelation," whether it's a word you hear in your head, or something someone speaks to you, or a dream you have—all other experiences are
judged under the truth of Scripture. What *has* God said? A lot:

You are my true son (1 John 3:1).
You are completely forgiven and cleansed (1 John 1:9).
Your sin nature has been removed (Romans 6:11; Colossians 2:11).
Christ is now your true life and nature (Ephesians 2:4–6; Galatians 2:20).
You have a new name (Isaiah 62:2; Revelation 2:17).

We also know that God speaks to us through the body of Christ. Men and
women who know you well—and even some who don't, but have a prophetic word
from God—they can help you hear your new name, or validate the name you've
heard God speak to you personally.

God *does* speak to us intimately and personally as well. He speaks through
movies and songs and life experiences. He speaks through dreams. And most
of all, he speaks in our hearts. When Jesus said, "My sheep listen to my voice,"
he meant it (John 10:27). Where does he speak to us? *In our hearts,* for that is
where Christ dwells (Ephesians 3:17). He will whisper words to you there. And
he will speak to you through your heart's *desires.* Who is the man you *want* to
be, what is the battle you want to have? That is your desire because that is who
you *are!*

Go ahead—embarrass yourself. What would you really love for God to say
to you?

WARNING!

The battle is going to get intense here. The Enemy, the Accuser, is not going to take this one lying down. This is the last thing he wants you to know. You will need to reject all accusation and fight off all discouragement and resignation. God may speak something immediately to you, and then confirm it over time with other "new names" and revelations of who you truly are as a man. Or, he may unfold this to you over the next few months. Don't be discouraged and don't give up. Hang in there—this is part of your warrior training.

WARNING!

Do you know what will be the hardest part of hearing your new name? Accepting it. Because what you *want* to hear is so very, very close to what you *will* hear, you'll think you're just making it up. If it sounds too good to be true, then it's probably true! Or did you think you could offer better gifts than God?

There is one other surprising source of our new name—our wound. For as we explored in chapter 5, those wounds were *aimed* at you, they were sent to take out your strength and so they reveal what your strength is. Because the Enemy arranges for our wound in a very specific, targeted way, it will help to reveal our calling and name. Charles was meant to be a musician—but his wound stopped him dead in his tracks. Reggie was meant to be a doctor—but his wound kept him from even attempting medical school. What has your wound prevented you from doing, or from trying, or from becoming over the years? This is a deep clue to who you really are.

It might help to know that the false self is never wholly false. What we do, you see, is find a few of our gifts and then we live off them and hide everything else. It's a false self in that it's not a whole self, a full picture of who you are. But even there, even in that misused strength, you will find something that is true of you.

DISPATCH

God said to me, "Do not be afraid of your heart, Dennis." What? What does that mean? As worship started I was asking God to tell me my name and what he thought of me. He began saying repeatedly, "You are not a failure! You are not a failure!" Ah . . . there it was. I knew there was a root, but did not know what it was. I totally agree that you must acknowledge your wound in order to begin the healing process. I grew up believing I was a failure. No matter how well I did in sports or just about anything else, it was never good enough. It hurt too much, so I buried

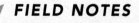 **FIELD NOTES**

WARNING!

As God does speak, WRITE IT DOWN, because it's all going to feel false in a day or two. The Enemy will rush in and try to steal it, or confuse you, or just make you forget. Write it down, and keep coming back to it, rereading what God gave you, and adding to it as he gives you more!

my heart. As I wept, God continued to pour his heart out to me. I could not write fast enough. One of the things he said was, "You are no longer a question mark." He also said, "You are a warrior, Dennis! You are a mighty warrior. I will use you to set the captives free."

A couple of weeks later an older couple from Australia ministered to us. I had joked about being part Maori (the native people of New Zealand known for their fierce warriors) and when they prayed for me, they declared they truly did see the warrior in me. I am beginning to receive God's view of me. I know he has a call on my life. I long to embrace it. I long to live from my heart and impact others.

DENNIS

Of course, all this means that we *reject the lie* as well, those deep lies that came in with our wound. No matter how true they might feel, God says they are lies. You are not alone, you are not a failure, you are not a mama's boy. Your new name is going to collide head-on with the lie that has been with you for a long time. Which are you going to believe? Better, *who* are you going to believe—the One who made you, or the father of lies?

Dearest Jesus, thank you for this great work you have begun in my heart. O take me deeper, Lord, deeper into healing, deeper into strength, deeper into my true name. Seal this work in my heart with your blood and let not one ounce be stolen from me. Carry me on, I pray in your name.

CHAPTER 8

A BATTLE TO FIGHT: THE ENEMY

If we would endeavor, like men of courage, to stand in the battle, surely we would feel the favorable assistance of God from heaven. For he who giveth us occasion to fight, to the end we may get the victory, is ready to succor those that fight manfully, and do trust in his grace.

THOMAS À KEMPIS

BEFORE SETTING OUT

Two things before you start working through this chapter:

Watch *Saving Private Ryan*. I know, the opening scenes in particular are horrific and tragic beyond words. But the stories of battle and valor, fear and cowardice are really, really powerful. Who do you want to be? Who would you hate to be? What's the best moment, and the worst moment for you in the movie?

Do you need to reread the chapter in the book?

GUT REACTION

What's your gut-level reaction to this chapter?

GETTING YOUR BEARINGS

The Goal

Over the next four chapters we are shifting from the healing of your masculine heart to the *release* of your heart into the Battle, the Adventure, and the Beauty. But we're going to start with the Battle. Why? Because (1) it's where most men get taken out *and*, (2) if you want the Beauty and the Adventure, you're going to have to fight for them! Our aim here is threefold: to recover our warrior heart, to uncover the Enemy and his tactics, and to learn some strategy for winning this war.

Trail Markers

- A man must have a battle to fight, a great mission for his life that involves but also transcends home and family.
- God *has* given you a place in the Great Battle, and your initiation journey *will* take you there.
- As a warrior, you must have *vision* and *cunning*.
- To beat the enemy called the flesh, you must embrace the promise of the New Covenant—that God has given you a new heart.

- To beat the enemy of the world, you must expose the counterfeits it offers you—counterfeit battles, adventures, and beauties.
- And as for Satan . . . you begin by bringing him back into your real beliefs and the way you evaluate life.

SETTING OUT

You need a battle to fight; you need a place for the warrior in you to come alive and be honed, trained, seasoned. If Bly is right (and I believe he is), that "the early death of a man's [internal warrior—his fierce side] keeps the boy in him from growing up," then the opposite is true—if we can reawaken that fierce quality in a man, hook it up to a higher purpose, release the warrior within, then the boy can grow up and become truly masculine.

What is your reaction to reading the letter on the opposite page?

DISPATCH

July 14, 1861
Camp Clark, Washington

My very dear Sarah:
The indications are very strong that we shall move in a few days—perhaps tomorrow. Lest I should not be able to write again, I feel impelled to write a few lines that may fall under your eye when I shall be no more . . .

I have no misgivings about, or lack of confidence in the cause to which I am engaged, and my courage does not halt or falter. I know how strongly American Civilization now leans on the triumph of the Government, and how great a debt we owe to those who went before us through the blood and sufferings of the

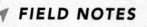

FIELD NOTES

Revolution. And I am willing—perfectly willing—to lay down all my joys in this life, to help maintain this Government, and to pay that debt . . .

Sarah, my love for you is deathless, it seems to bind me with mighty cables that nothing but Omnipotence could break; and yet my love of Country comes over me like a strong wind and bears me unresistably on with all these chains to the battle field.

The memories of the blissful moments I have spent with you come creeping over me, and I feel most gratified to God and to you that I have enjoyed them so long. And hard it is for me to give them up and burn to ashes the hopes of future years when, God willing, we might still have lived and loved together, and seen our sons grown up to honorable manhood around us. I have, I know, but few and small claims upon Divine Providence, but something whispers to me—perhaps it is the wafted prayer of my little Edgar, that I shall return to my loved ones unharmed. If I do not, my dear Sarah, never forget how much I loved you, and when my last breath escapes me on the battlefield, it will whisper your name. Forgive my many faults, and the many pains I have caused you. How thoughtless and foolish I have many times been! How gladly would I wash out with my tears every little spot upon your happiness.

But O Sarah! If the dead can come back to this earth and flit unseen around those they loved, I shall always be near you; in the gladdest days and in the darkest nights . . . always, always, and if there be a soft breeze upon your cheek, it shall be my breath, as the cool air fans your throbbing temple, it shall be my spirit passing by. Sarah, do not mourn me dead; think I am gone and wait for thee, for we shall meet again.

(SULLIVAN BALLOU WAS KILLED IN THE FIRST BATTLE OF BULL RUN.)

And, seeing his fierce love for Sarah, what drove Sullivan Ballou to the battlefield? Have you ever felt something similar in your heart?

"I'd love to be William Wallace, leading the charge with a big sword in my hand," sighed a friend, "but I feel like I'm the guy back there in the fourth row, with a hoe." Most of the men I talk to feel this way, especially at the outset of their masculine journey. The warrior longing is there, but it's mingled with other voices—voices of fear, doubt, confusion, or resignation—voices that tend to drown out the warrior heart. Two questions for you: Do you truly believe, down in your gut, that you *are* William Wallace in your life—that God has called you to a crucial front line and that you have the warrior heart required for the battle? If the answer is yes!, tell me who gave that to you. If the answer is *no*, or *I have my doubts*, tell me who told you that.

Earlier in the book I said that the reason the Enemy fired all those arrows at your heart is *because he fears you*. Can you allow for a moment that that might be true— that these very doubts you now wrestle with telling you you aren't dangerous, you'll never be a great warrior with a true battle, are in fact *lies*? What does that possibility arouse in you?

Think again about the films you love—*Braveheart, Rocky, Fury, Private Ryan*. How many of them are stories of ordinary guys—underdogs, really—who finally step up into their true strength and engage? (For example, did William Wallace see himself as the liberator of Scotland at the start of his adult life? What was his

plan when he came back to Scotland as a grown man—wasn't it to be a farmer?) For that matter, how many of the biblical stories are also "underdog" themes?

FROM THE MAP

The LORD is with you, mighty warrior.

JUDGES 6:12

When the angel of the Lord saluted Gideon as a mighty warrior, do you know who Gideon was and what he happened to be doing? Gideon was—at least in his own eyes—a loser from the biggest family of losers, the youngest lad in a family known for its weakness. And he was at that moment threshing his wheat down in a hole, terrified of even being *noticed* by his enemies (Judges 6:11–15).

You might also recall that remarkable showdown the prophet Elijah had with the prophets of Baal—at the conclusion of which he had 450 of them slaughtered on the spot (a scene not unlike one out of Braveheart, I might add). After the stunning victory what did Elijah do? He ran for his life and hid in a cave (1 Kings 18–19).

Then there is King David, who faced more battles and killed more men in hand-to-hand combat than we can count. That fierce warrior describes himself in the Psalms as a "leaning wall" and a "tottering fence" about to fall over with the next strong wind (Psalm 62:3).

It's just possible that your own self-estimation may not be very accurate, either.

And what are those stories trying to get across to you about your life?

In your life you are William Wallace—who else could be? There is no other man who can replace you in your life, in the arena you've been called to. If you leave your place in the line, it will remain empty. No one else can be who you are meant to be. If you do not fight for the people in your life—your family and friends—then who will fight for them? If you do not step up into the battle God has for you, who will take your place? (Another man cannot, for to take your place he would have to leave his place in the line.)

WARRIORS AND MERCENARIES

I think we could probably divide all the guys in the world into three categories:

1. Guys who have no battle ("fourth row back with a hoe" kind of guys)
2. Guys who have a battle but it's the wrong one (King Saul trying to kill David)
3. Guys who truly know their place in the Battle

Think about some actual guys you work with or go to church with. Place them in one of these categories.

Mercenaries are guys who are hired to fight, guys who have no stake in the battle at hand except a paycheck. They are fighting the wrong battle or for the wrong reason, or both. After all, Saul (prior to becoming Paul) thought he was fighting the right battle before that little incident on the Damascus road. And King Saul (is it something in the name?!) was certain it was his God-given mission to kill

David. If you feel that you are in the right battle, are you willing to test that a bit? Take a moment to define your battle:

What is it over? What's at stake?

And who is your adversary, your enemy? Meaning, who are most of your aggressive energies *really* aimed at in the course of a week?

And how does that tie into God's Great Battle—the one described in Isaiah 61:1–3? Who called you to this battle?

How much prayer and reflection went into your investing yourself here—the place you are fighting and the way you are fighting?

And how desperately do you need God to show up for any chance of victory? Is that how you pray about it? Really?

FROM THE MAP

Or suppose a king is about to go to war against another king. Won't he first sit down and consider whether he is able . . . ?

LUKE 14:31

An unreflective man is a dangerous man . . . to himself and to his own side.

If you win the battles you are currently fighting, what will be the result? What will that bring you?

Is there a godly man in your life who agrees with your understanding of what you've laid out here?

A man must have a battle to fight, a great mission to his life that involves and yet transcends even home and family. He must have a cause to which he is devoted even unto death, for this is written into the fabric of his being. Listen carefully now: YOU DO. That is why God created you—to be his intimate *ally*, to join him in the Great Battle. You have a specific place in the line, a mission God made you for. That is why it is so essential to hear from God about your true name, because in that name is the mission of your life. Churchill was called upon to lead the British through the desperate hours of World War II. He said, "I felt as if I were walking with destiny, and that all my past life had been but a preparation for this hour and for this trial."

The same is true of you; *you* are "walking with destiny" and all *your* life "has been preparation for this hour and for this trial." Do you have any sense of what that preparation has been, and what your Great Battle might be?

What issue gets you riled up, makes you pound your fist on the table? What cause or issue really gets your attention when somebody brings it up?

And what does that issue or cause represent to you? Why do you get upset over it?

OUR ENEMY—THE FLESH

Having a vision is only part of our warrior training. The second quality of a warrior's life is *cunning*—knowing when to fight and when to run, knowing what weapons to use and when. Knowing your enemy and how he works is essential wisdom for any warrior. How would you live if you knew that there was a group of terrorists sent into the U.S. to take you out? That's the mentality that breeds a kind of daily cunning.

We'll start with the flesh, partly because that tends to be the only enemy the church really talks about much. Unfortunately, what is often taught does more harm than good. (You'll see why in a minute.) Remember, when I use the term *flesh* I am referring not to our physical body but to our "sin nature," or what the Scripture calls our "old man." Given all the honest self-assessment we've done through the guide up to this point, how would you describe your own "flesh" these days—in terms that are specific to you? Who is the poser that is your "flesh"?

 **FIELD NOTES**

WARNING!

Our place in God's Battle and our life mission is something that grows over time and comes with greater clarity only over time. Don't be discouraged or deceived if you don't see it with total clarity now. A HUGE part of our battle is seeing it with clarity, and that is something the Enemy continually tries to muddy and cloud. The clarity itself is something you have to fight for!

John Owen called the flesh "the traitor within," ready to drop the drawbridge and betray us at a moment's notice. Do you have a growing awareness of how your flesh would like to betray you—or sabotage your strength—when it comes to . . .

The Battle?

The Adventure?

The Beauty?

THE NEW HEART

Okay, now for one of the biggest issues we'll ever come to terms with, as big as our wound or our new name or even facing the enemy. Is your flesh the real you? Are you a sinner at the core? What have you been taught about that?

FROM THE MAP

In Jeremiah 17:9, God describes the condition of the fallen human heart:

The heart is deceitful above all things and beyond cure.
Who can understand it?

Clear enough. Man in his fallen state, man separated from God, has a wicked heart. But later in that same book, in Jeremiah 31, God promises to remedy the condition of the human heart with a brand-new arrangement:

"The time is coming," declares the LORD,
　　"when I will make a new covenant
with the people of Israel
　　and with the people of Judah.
It will not be like the covenant
　　I made with their ancestors
when I took them by the hand
　　to lead them out of Egypt,
because they broke my covenant,
　　though I was a husband to them," declares the LORD.
"This is the covenant I will make with the people of Israel
　　after that time," declares the LORD.
"I will put my law in their minds
　　and write it on their hearts.
I will be their God
　　and they will be my people." (verses 31–33)

And in Ezekiel 36 God reiterates that promise of a new covenant, a new arrangement with mankind: "I will give you a new heart and put a new spirit in you; I will remove from you your heart of stone [your stubborn, rebellious heart] and give you a heart of flesh [a heart supple to me, tender to my ways]. And I will put my Spirit in you and move you to follow my decrees and be careful to keep my laws" (verses 26–27).

So what exactly is the promise of the New Covenant? How does God plan to deal with the fallen human heart?

FROM THE MAP

The New Testament is the record of God keeping his promise. It details the New Covenant he offers to man and all that means for our lives. In his writings especially, Paul lays out slowly and clearly the doctrine of the New Covenant, and what Christ has accomplished for us:

> God made him who had no sin to be sin for us, so that in him we might become the righteousness of God. (2 Corinthians 5:21)

> A man is not a Jew if he is only one outwardly, nor is circumcision merely outward and physical. No, a man is a Jew if he is one inwardly; and circumcision is circumcision of the heart, by the Spirit, not by the written code. (Romans 2:28–29 NIV 84)

> In [Christ] you were also circumcised, *in the putting off of the sinful nature*, not with a circumcision done by the hands of men but with the circumcision done by Christ . . . (Colossians 2:11, emphasis added)

> Now if we died with Christ, we believe that we will also live with him. For we know that since Christ was raised from the dead, he cannot die again; death no longer has mastery over him. The death he died, he died to sin once for all; but the life he lives, he lives to God. In the same way, count yourselves dead to sin but alive to God in Christ Jesus. (Romans 6:8–11)

FROM THE MAP

I do not understand what I do. For what I want to do I do not do, but what I hate I do. And if I do what I do not want to do, I agree that the law is good. As it is, *it is no longer I myself who do it*, but it is sin living in me.

For I know that good itself does not dwell in me, that is, *in my sinful nature*. For I have the desire to do what is good, but I cannot carry it out. For I do not do the good I want to do, but the evil I do not want to do—this I keep on doing. Now if I do what I do not want to do, *it is no longer I who do it, but it is sin living in me that does it.*

ROMANS 7:15–20,
emphasis added

Christ's righteousness is now ours. Most of us have been told that in some way. But is that righteousness only *positional*, having to do with our standing before God? Or is it also *actual*, changing our very nature as well? According to these passages, this new, spiritual circumcision did what for our heart, removed what? What is Paul's conclusion for us—what has God done to our hearts and what are we therefore to count as true about ourselves?

What about our sin? Don't we still face a battle against the flesh? Indeed we do. But you can't hope to win that battle if you believe that your flesh is the real you, that you are still by nature a sinner. Listen again to Paul:

What distinction is Paul making here about his true desires and his sinful nature? Does he see them as one and the same?

And which part does Paul believe is most true about him as a new man in Christ?

Where does Christ dwell in a man who believes in him? And is it possible that the part of our heart which Christ dwells in is evil?

FIELD NOTES

FROM THE MAP

I pray that out of [God's] glorious riches he may strengthen you with power through his Spirit in your inner being, so that Christ may dwell in your hearts through faith.

EPHESIANS 3:16–17

There is only one conclusion we can draw from the New Covenant and all God has done for us in and through Christ . . . it is that very conclusion Paul himself comes to in Romans 8:

The real you is on the side of God against the false self. Knowing this makes all the difference in the world. Linger over this for a moment—how would believing that your true heart is for God, and is one with Christ, and therefore is good . . . how would that change the way you approach life?

No, your flesh is your *false self* and the only way to deal with it is to crucify it. Now follow me very closely here: We are never, ever told to crucify our heart. We are never told to kill the true man within us, never told to get rid of those deep desires for battle, adventure, and beauty. We are told to shoot the traitor. How? Choose against him every time you see him rouse his ugly head. Walk right into those situations you normally run from. Speak right to the issues you normally remain silent about. If you want to grow in true masculine strength, then you must stop sabotaging yours.

Do you ever send a steak back because it isn't cooked right? It's time to send one back.

Do you ever speak up in a meeting at work or at church? It's time to speak up.

Do you ever ask your wife how she's feeling, even though you have no idea what to do with what she might say? It's time to ask her.

Have you opened up to a good buddy about this whole process you're going through and spoken honestly about your life? It's time to open up.

How else can you stop sabotaging and start letting your strength arrive?

FIELD NOTES

FROM THE MAP

A new power is in operation. The Spirit of life in Christ, like a strong wind, has magnificently cleared the air, freeing you from a fated lifetime of brutal tyranny at the hands of sin and death . . . Anyone, of course, who has not welcomed this invisible but clearly present God, the Spirit of Christ, won't know what we're talking about. But for you who welcome him, in whom he dwells . . . if the alive-and-present God who raised Jesus from the dead moves into your life, he'll do the same thing in you that he did in Jesus . . . When God lives and breathes in you (and he does, as surely as he did in Jesus), you are delivered from that dead life. (THE MESSAGE)

LETTING OUR STRENGTH SHOW UP

We must let our strength show up. It seems so strange, after all this, that a man would not allow his strength to arrive, but many of us are unnerved by our own masculinity. What will happen if we really let it out? What do you *fear* will happen?

One thing we know: Nothing will ever be the same. What might change if you really let your masculine heart and your true strength show up . . .

At work?

At home?

At church?

OUR ENEMY—THE WORLD

The world is a carnival of counterfeits—counterfeit battles (we've talked about those), counterfeit adventures, counterfeit beauties. Where have you been suckered by the world in the past? And how about now—where do you hear it seducing you nowadays?

Men should think of it as a corruption of their strength. The world offers a man a false sense of power and security. Where does your sense of power come from most of the time? Is it how well you're doing, or what you know, or what others think of you, how they treat you? Is it a position or a title you carry, a pulpit you stand behind or a white coat?

Where do you feel strongly pulled to turn for a sense of validation as a man? What is calling to you, promising you that?

A BREAK IN THE CLOUDS

I know we've said it before, it bears repeating: Most men struggle with lust and porn and counterfeit beauties *not because of sex* but because they are desperately seeking *validation as a man.*

I told you about Carl, and how he had given his strength away to women so many times. That particular kind of sabotage brings a very deep kind of bondage, and it requires careful surgery. What follows is the prayer I used with Carl—and

DISPATCH

I did this the other night—asked myself what I'm so afraid will happen if I really let my heart and my strength show up. (I edit myself a lot when I'm around others. I keep my heart in a box.) Then I just wrote down what came to me. "I'm afraid I'll start taking heads off. I'm afraid I'll rip the clothes off some beautiful woman. I'm afraid I'll go off on some wild, harebrained adventure." There it is—all three core longings. And the lie I saw is that Christ has not made my heart new, so I can't really let it out for the true version of those things.

JOHN

WARNING!

I said we should let people feel the weight of who we are, and let them deal with it. By that I do not mean we become belligerent or recklessly destructive with our current situation. What I mean by letting people feel the weight of who we are is that we come out from hiding, stop apologizing that we have a wild heart, stop editing ourselves to fit neatly within a world of posers. Many things are probably calling for a change. Much of our present life was built by and for a poser, and when the poser changes, his world will change as well. But remember that a warrior uses *cunning*. Pick your battles; don't become an early casualty because of reckless abandon.

many others—to break the bonds created by sexual sin. I include it because many of you are going to find it helpful.

> *Lord Jesus, you made me a sexual being and made sexuality to be good and holy. Forgive me for abusing your creation, for all of my sexual sins with [her name]. I took something that was not mine to take and I gave away something that was not hers to have. Forgive me, Lord. I bring all these sins under your cross and your atonement. Wash us both with your blood. And by your cross I break all soul ties and all bonds with [name] which were created through those sexual acts. For by your cross I am crucified now to [her name] and she is crucified to me (Galatians 6:14). I release her to you totally, and ask you to restore her to you. I once again present my body and my sexuality to you as a living sacrifice (Romans 12:1) to be your holy temple. By the cross and blood of Jesus, I cancel all claims that Satan has gained to me through my sins (Colossians 2:13–15). Jesus, restore my strength, restore my heart, restore my sexuality in a holy bond with you, and you alone. I pray this in the mighty name of Jesus.*

The world of posers is shaken by a real man. They'll do whatever it takes to get you back in line—threaten you, bribe you, seduce you, undermine you. They crucified Jesus. But it didn't work, did it? You must let your strength show up. Remember Christ in the Garden of Gethsemane, the sheer force of his presence? Many of us have actually been afraid to let our strength show up because the world doesn't have a place for it. Fine. The world's screwed up. Let people feel the weight of who you are and let them deal with it.

What do you expect the reaction is going to be . . .

At work?

At home?

At church?

And what about a false sense of security? I asked you to put down the book for a few moments and consider what you would think of yourself if tomorrow you lost everything that the world has rewarded you for. Do that now—what do you fear losing, and what would you feel about yourself if you did lose it all?

THE DEVIL

Now for the enemy we have been taught the least about—Satan. We'll deal with him in the next chapter, but let me pose a few questions here, to prime the pump. What was your reaction to my narrative about the traffic jam with Stasi, and the "conversation" that went on in my head? Have you experienced anything like that? Did it even occur to you that it involved your Enemy, or do you pretty much write those moments off as your struggle with yourself?

Really now—does Satan have any place in your actual thinking? What event in your life, what arrow or temptation, what thought or occurrence have you attributed to him this week? This month? This year? Name five things.

Oh . . . and how about your work here in this field guide—has everything been going smoothly? No fears, no confusion, no doubts? Has Satan been at work at all against you here?

Strengthen me, with your strength, O God. Rally my soul into this great battle. Dear Jesus, expose the enemies of my heart and my life so that I may see the battle lines more clearly. Show me my place, speak again to me my name. Grant me a vision for my life, and grant me the cunning of a warrior. Sustain me in this battle and in this journey, that in your name I might gain the victory. I pray in the mighty power of Jesus' name.

CHAPTER 9

A BATTLE TO FIGHT: THE STRATEGY

As part of Christ's army, you march in the ranks of
gallant spirits. Every one of your fellow soldiers is the child of a King.
Some, like you, are in the midst of battle, besieged on every side
by affliction and temptation. Others, after many assaults, repulses,
and rallyings of their faith, are already standing upon the wall of heaven
as conquerors. From there they look down and urge you, their comrades
on earth, to march up the hill after them. This is their cry: "Fight to the
death and the City is your own, as now it is ours!"

WILLIAM GURNALL

BEFORE SETTING OUT

Two things before you start working through this chapter:

Watch *The Matrix* (the first film in the series). The movie is a stunning portrayal of the Battle, with astounding insights into the three ways the Enemy works. First, Neo doesn't even know the Matrix is there—he thinks the "real" world is the only reality there is. Second, once he does wake up to the Matrix and its Agents, they try to intimidate him back into line. Third, he resists, and they offer to cut him a deal. And notice that their attack is always against his true name (!).

I also want you to do something we rarely do—I want you to *pay attention* for one day to the thoughts that go through your head, the "voices" that are speaking to you, at you, in the course of a single day. *Tune in* to what goes on when you wake up, when you talk to your wife, when you go to work, when you see a beautiful woman, when someone criticizes you—all the events of a normal day.

GUT REACTION

What are you really struck by? What did this chapter make you want to do?

GETTING YOUR BEARINGS

The Goal

In the masculine journey a man needs three things: (1) He needs to get his heart back. (2) He needs to know his place in the battle. (3) He needs to know how to fight. Your goal here is learning something of #3—how to fight in a spiritual war.

Trail Markers

- Stage One of Satan's strategy is always "I'm not here—this is just you." Most men live their whole life duped at that level.
- In Stage Two Satan moves to intimidation—trying to threaten us back in line.
- At Stage Three he offers us a deal of some kind.
- We've been given our aggressive heart to fight aggressively.
- And God has provided the weapons we need.
- The kingdom of heaven suffers violence, and violent men take it by force.

STAGE ONE: "I'M NOT HERE"

What was your reaction to the true story from D Day, about the paratroopers who hid themselves in a farmhouse and got drunk on the night of one of the most important battles in the history of mankind?

These men *knew* they were at war, yet they refused to act like it. They lived in a dangerous denial—a denial that not only endangered them but countless others who depended on them to do their part. I believe it is a *perfect* picture of the Western church when it comes to spiritual warfare. Do you think I exaggerate? Name three men you know who take Satan seriously—who talk openly about his schemes as if they were monitoring the movements of a terrorist group, and who pray out loud directly against him on a regular basis.

What is God saying through Peter and James that we must do in our battle against the devil? Is that a passive thing or an aggressive thing? Which part of your heart does that engage, call up, require?

FIELD NOTES

Be self-controlled and alert. Your enemy the devil prowls around like a roaring lion looking for someone to devour. *Resist him*, standing firm in the faith, because you know that your brothers throughout the world are undergoing the same kind of sufferings.

1 PETER 5:8–9 NIV 84
(emphasis added)

Submit yourselves, then, to God. *Resist the devil*, and he will flee from you.

JAMES 4:7
(emphasis added)

Let's start with some exposure. I said that the Enemy always tries to jam the lines of communication. My first example was in marriage, but it applies to good friendships as well. Do you ever experience that sense of *accusation* in your marriage or key friendships, that feeling that you're just not measuring up?

What about during prayer—are you able to focus without any interruptions, without any thoughts distracting you? Do this exercise today or tomorrow: Notice what goes on in your thoughts during your prayer time; notice every thought that interferes or distracts or discourages or condemns. What do you discover? Write it down.

Many, many times I've come under a cloak of *confusion* so thick I suddenly find myself wondering why I ever believed in Jesus in the first place. That sweet communion I normally enjoy with God is cut off, gone, vanished like the sun behind a cloud. If you don't know what's up, you'll think you really have lost your faith or been abandoned by God or whatever spin the Enemy puts on it. Has that ever happened to you—that cloud of confusion, or doubt, or a faithless, "where is God?" kind of feeling? Does it happen on a regular basis? Has it happened at any point during your work through this guide? Who did you blame that on?

Satan is constantly putting his spin on things. Oh, if we would see this more clearly, what freedom it would bring! The episode I described in the last chapter, when Stasi and I were in the car and I went through that little inner dialogue that led to "divorce"—has anything like that happened to you recently?

Do you find yourself coming to conclusions about what another person is thinking or feeling toward you? Right now, write down what you think your wife, your boss, and your closest friend thinks about you these days, then ask yourself, *Have they actually said that to me, or is that just what I kind of "sense" is going on?*

Wife

Boss

Friend

Satan is called the accuser of the brethren (Revelation 12:10) for a reason. So long as a man remains no real threat, Satan's line to him is *You're fine*. But after you do take sides, it becomes *Your heart is bad and you know it*. His deepest and most crippling attacks are always accusations against our heart, our identity, our new name. We've *got* to see this more clearly, expose it. Think of what goes on—what you hear and feel—when you really blow it. Recall a recent event—or better still, observe it happening this week. Write down what you normally just let play through your head.

Examples: *I'm such an idiot; I always do that; I'll never amount to anything.*

How about when you're really going to step forward as a man? Have you taken any steps forward as a result of your work in this guide? What kind of accusation did you hear (are you hearing now)?

Examples: *Who are you kidding? This may be for some guys, but not you. You're making all this up. Sure—give it a try. You'll fail eventually.*

What are the sentences about yourself that you've been hearing for years? How have you felt, in a personal way, that your heart is bad and you know it?

Examples: *I'm basically a slob; I'm a lustful man to the core; I'm arrogant and self-centered; bottom line about me is, I'm a coward.*

We've got to stop making agreements with the Enemy. I explained that Satan will come looking for a weakness in our defenses. He will throw a thought or a temptation at us in hopes that we will swallow it. He knows your story, knows what works with you and so the line is tailor-made to your situation. If we make an agreement, if something in our heart says, *Yeah, you're right*, then he pours it on. Let that go on for years, and you've given him a stronghold.

What agreements have you been making with the Enemy's lies? Can you name them? Have you been agreeing with what you thought others were thinking of you? Or with those sentences you hear when you blow it? With the accusation that your heart is not good? What else?

DISPATCH

I knew I was going to face a battle, but I had no idea how hard the Enemy was going to hit. I had been invited by a good friend of mine to join him in a retreat he was leading and to do whatever I wished: to just relax, to take it in, or to take part. I knew that this would challenge me with one of my greatest fears: being with a group of people without a clearly established place for me—not requiring any of my gifts, talents, or knowledge, only my presence, which I wasn't comfortable with.

At one point, one of the girls in the group asked for prayer. We circled around her. As she shared her heartbreak over the words spoken and unspoken to her by her father, I felt intense condemnation and despair that this is what I am doing to my teenage daughter. In a matter of moments, I left the circle and the room out of a feeling of suffocation over my failure as a father.

I grabbed my keys and left the ranch not knowing what I would do or if I would return. As I drove off I found myself crying uncontrollably and then shouting at the top of my lungs, "you @#$% idiot." I pleaded for God to help me. Immediately, he brought to my mind all the times I had yelled those same words in self-hatred for not being able to "do things right." That had become the explanation for my "fail-ures." I was simply an idiot. Throughout my life, I had agreed with this message, believing it was probably the truest thing about me. I lived carefully and worked hard to overcome who I was or to at least not be exposed through failure. It wasn't until that moment that I realized the "you" in the accusation was coming *at* me and not *from* me. So I renounced this accusation each time I had made it and announced God's truth of who I was.

GARY

Break those agreements now.

> *Dear Jesus, forgive me for making these agreements with the Enemy. Forgive me for giving him ground in my life. I break those agreements now. I break all agreements with [get specific here—name them] and I renounce the lie. I cancel any ground I have given Satan in my life, and I make all agreements with you, Lord Jesus. You are the Way and the Truth and the Life; all the ground that I once gave to Satan I now give to you and you alone. In the authority of your name I pray.*

HANGING ON TO THE TRUTH

Yet we must be watchful, especially in the beginning of the temptation; for the enemy is then more easily overcome, if he is not suffered to enter the door of our hearts, but is resisted without the gate at his first knock.

Thomas À Kempis

You're just not going to be able to live an ordinary life anymore. I'm sorry. But you know too much now. You are too dangerous to leave alone, and the Enemy is going to come after you, to try to put you back in your place.

The battle can get ugly. He doesn't just pour on the accusation and tempta-tion; Satan can pour on *feelings*, too. He'll do everything he can to get you to think and feel as if what he says is the bottom-line truth. Walk into a dark house late at night, and suddenly fear sweeps over you; or just stand in a grocery store checkout line with all those tabloids shouting sex at you, and suddenly lust is all over you.

But this is where your strength is revealed and increased through exercise. Stand on what is true and do not let go. Period. No matter what you may feel. Remember the scene in *Braveheart* where Robert the Bruce's evil father is whispering lies to him about treason and compromise? He says to Robert what the Enemy says to us in a thousand ways: "All men betray; all men lose heart." How does Robert answer? He yells back,

> I don't want to lose heart!
> I want to believe, like [Wallace] does.
> I will never be on the wrong side again.

That is the turning point in his life . . . and in ours. Okay, maybe you can't yell back in a staff meeting, but you can in your prayer closet—or in the car! You need to start swinging back. Right now, right here, I want you to write down what is true about you according to Scripture and according to those personal words God has spoken to you. Who are you, *really*?

A BREAK IN THE CLOUDS

In the film *The Matrix*, the hero is an ordinary guy who lives a pretty ordinary life as a programmer for a large software corporation. In the "real" world, the world of going to work and paying taxes and eating noodles at a Chinese restaurant, he is simply Thomas Anderson. "Nobody special," in his own words.

But he discovers that the *real* world is a lot bigger than he thought; that in fact he is caught up in a supernatural battle against sinister forces (the Agents) who

DISPATCH

Thank you for the call to spiritual warfare. I cut my teeth on that in my early Christian days . . . but we sure haven't been practicing it. There is no question in my mind that we have been under immense attack. I will fight back in the power of the Lord.

MAC

control what he thought was the "real" world through deception and intimidation. He gets a new name, Neo, and a new identity and a much more dangerous role in the story.

The beginning of the end for the Agents takes place in a subway station showdown. Up to this point everyone has always run from the Agents. Neo is about to, but then he turns to face them. Watching from the world beyond the world, one of his fellow warriors turns in amazement to their leader. She asks, "What is he doing?" Smiling, the leader says, "He's beginning to believe." Believe what? *Who he is*.

A brutal battle ensues, throughout which the Agent keeps calling him "Mr. Anderson"—in a sneering and condemning *who do you think you are?* kind of way. Just when it looks as though the devil will win, the hero musters his last bit of strength and says, "My name is Neo," and with that he delivers the winning blow.

Bottom Line: We answer Satan's Stage One with "You are here, and I'm sick of you blaming everything on me. I am onto your schemes."

STAGE TWO: INTIMIDATION

The next level of the Enemy's strategy is intimidation. When we begin to question him, to resist his lies, to see his hand in the "ordinary trials" of our lives, then he steps up the attack; he turns to intimidation and fear. He's going to try to keep you from taking a stand. He moves from subtle seduction to open assault. The thoughts come crashing in; all sorts of stuff begin to fall apart in your life; your faith seems paper thin.

Has anything gone wrong in your life since you began work in this guide? What happened? Did you see the Enemy's hand in it? How have you responded?

REALLY?

What can Satan cause, I mean, really? Most men would admit that the devil is probably behind some of the temptation and maybe the accusation in their lives. But that's about it. Let's look at what the Bible says Satan can cause.

PHYSICAL AFFLICTION

There's the story of the woman in the synagogue who couldn't even stand up straight, "who had been crippled by a spirit for eighteen years. She was bent over and could not straighten up at all" (Luke 13:11). And dare we forget Job, who experienced "painful sores from the soles of his feet to the crown of his head" as a direct result of Satan's attack (Job 2:7). Jesus healed a mute boy and a blind man by *kicking out a demon* (Mark 9:14–26; Matthew 12:22).

FINANCIAL AFFLICTION

Who was behind the Chaldean raid on Job's herds, an event that wiped him out financially? Satan, clearly (Job 1:12, 17).

SPIRITUAL DOUBT, DISCOURAGEMENT, DISBELIEF

Paul says that Satan has "blinded the minds of unbelievers" (2 Cor. 4:4). But his work doesn't stop with non-Christians. Acts 5 recounts the story of Ananias and Sapphira, believers whose hearts were moved by Satan to lie to the elders of their church. Who is responsible for your inability to concentrate during prayer, or church, or Bible study? And how about "unanswered" prayer? Daniel 10 tells the story of how an angel of God was delayed *three weeks* from getting through to Daniel because of spiritual warfare! I'll bet Daniel just thought his prayers weren't effective (see Dan. 10:1–14).

RELATIONAL DISTRESS AND CONFLICT

Paul warns in Ephesians 4:26–27 that unresolved anger (as but one example) can give the devil a "stronghold."

FIELD NOTES

I'm really surprised at the number of men who think that this battle is going to be easy. They wonder why the Enemy doesn't run away at the first sign of our resistance. Yes, Scripture says that if we resist the devil, he will flee from us (James 4:7). And he will, but there is sometimes quite a battle wrapped up in that word *resist*. (Look at "From the Map" on the next page.) All that *aggression* God put in you, the desire to take heads off when you're mad, the joy of whacking something into kingdom come, our heart for battle—that's what's needed here. This is what it's for—aggressive spiritual warfare.

Bottom Line: Our answer to Satan for Stage Two is, "I'm not giving up and I'm not going away. *You* are the one that has to flee."

STAGE THREE: CUTTING A DEAL

After a round or two of intimidation, Satan then offers us a deal. He'll "suggest" to you through thoughts and feelings—sometimes through the words of another person—that your life would be easier if you just backed off.

In fact, some of you reading this now have already begun to have "second thoughts" about this chapter. You've heard or thought something like this: *I don't know about all this spiritual warfare stuff. None of the guys I know are fighting it. This seems a little extreme. I think I'll just focus on the Adventure.* Or maybe something like: *I know what my battles are and they aren't about Satan at all—they're with [my wife, my boss, my in-laws]. That's where the battle is.*

You are being encouraged to back off any real resisting of the devil (in direct contradiction to Scripture, which tells you to resist). Do you see how this works?

Has the Enemy offered you a deal you've been able to identify? Has there been a thought or a feeling to back off some arena of your life—or to get yourself a "little pleasure on the side"?

Persisting to the end will be the burr under your saddle—the thorn in your flesh—when the road ahead seems endless and your soul begs an early discharge. It weighs down every other difficulty of your calling. We have known many who have joined the army of Christ and like being a soldier for a battle or two, but have soon had enough and ended up deserting. They impulsively enlist for Christian duties . . . and are just as easily persuaded to lay it down. Like the new moon, they shine a little in the first part of the evening, but go down before the night is over.

William Gurnall

Bottom Line: Our answer for Stage Three is, "No deals. My heart and my loyalty belong to God. I am in this for the duration."

FROM THE MAP

When Jesus encounters the man in the tombs, he commands the demon to come out of him. *Nothing happens!* Jesus has to get more information, in this case, the demon's name (Legion) and his strength. Only after round two of battle is the man set free (Luke 8:26–33). And this is *Jesus* doing the commanding!

There's the man in the synagogue possessed by an evil spirit, who starts shouting that Jesus is the Holy One of God. Jesus has to rebuke him in a stern voice (Luke 4:35). Good grief—if Jesus had to get downright aggressive with these guys, do you think we'll need to say more than a quick prayer?

God gave you a will, and he gave you his authority so you will use it. You are to resist. I've heard many men pray something halfhearted like, "Jesus, would you bind Satan away from me?" Jesus told you to do it: "I have given you authority . . . to overcome all the power of the [evil one]" (Luke 10:19). Be *aggressive*—get tough with these guys.

THE WEAPONS OF WAR

This is a real war we're talking about. Men have been taken out right and left. "Do not be afraid of what you are about to suffer. I tell you, the devil will put some of you in prison to test you, and you will suffer persecution for ten days. Be faithful, even to the point of death, and I will give you life as your victor's crown" (Revelation 2:10). Remember, it's not *Home Improvement* you are in here—it's *Saving Private Ryan*. If you want to survive, better still, if you want to prevail, you're going to need several things:

A BREAK IN THE CLOUDS

There's a perfect picture of cutting a deal with the enemy in *The Matrix*. One of Neo's comrades, Cipher, has decided he's had it with the battle. It's just been too long and too hard. The enemy buys him off, he wines and dines him and promises to make him rich and famous. Cipher agrees, on the condition that he remembers nothing. It's a haunting scene because it's played out in the lives of men every day.

INTIMACY WITH GOD

Most men have a hard time sustaining any sort of devotional life because it has no vital connection to recovering and protecting their strength; it feels about as important as flossing. Hasn't it felt that way to you? On a scale of 1 to 10, with 1 being the thrill of flossing and 10 being great sex, where would you put your "quiet time," your devotional life?

We do not give a halfhearted attempt at the spiritual disciplines because we ought to, we do it because *we are history if we don't*. We've got to keep those lines of communication open, so use whatever helps. Sometimes I'll listen to music; other times I'll read Scripture or a passage from a book; often I will journal; maybe I'll go for a run; then there are those days when all I need is silence and solitude and the rising sun. The point is simply to *do whatever brings you back to your heart and the heart of God*.

Can you think of some times in the past that were rich with God? What were you doing?

Do *that* for your devotions.

INTIMACY WITH OTHERS

Don't even *think* about going into battle alone. Don't even try to take the masculine journey without at least one man by your side. The church understands that a man needs other men now, but what we've been offered is a two-dimensional solution: "accountability" groups or partners. Ugh. That sounds so Old Covenant: "You're really a fool and you're just waiting to rush into sin, so we'd better post a guard by you to keep you in line."

We don't need accountability groups; we need fellow *warriors*, someone to fight alongside us, someone to watch our back. We don't need a meeting of Really Nice Guys; we need a gathering of Really Dangerous Men.

A BREAK IN THE CLOUDS

Do you recall the scene in *Gladiator*, where Maximus and his men are facing their first major battle in the coliseum in Rome? They are sent into the arena to face they know not what. Waiting for the gates to open and an unknown enemy to rush upon them, Maximus says, "Whatever comes through those gates, we've got a better chance of surviving if we work together." The guys who ignore him and try it singlehandedly get taken out. Those who stick together, "contending as one man" (Philippians 1:27 NIV 84), are the ones who win the stunning upset.

Name one or two guys whom you'd want to gather with to fight for each other. Will you approach them and raise the idea? And if you can't think of anyone, if all the men you know are posers, then start *praying* for allies.

You might start with the suggestion to go through this guide together. Watch the films together, talk about them. Or get out together, share an adventure. Whatever you do, get out from under the religious veil, the suffocating atmosphere of posers acting spiritual. Be honest; be men.

THE ARMOR OF GOD

Okay, God has given you the armor. Wear it. Daily. Start by praying it on, as I laid out on page 173 in *Wild at Heart*.

THE AUTHORITY OF CHRIST

ALL of our victory in this life comes through what Christ has already accomplished for us in his death, his resurrection, and his ascension.

- The Cross: Cleanses us from sin, removes our old nature, and disarms the demons (Galatians 2:20; Colossians 2:13–15).
- The Resurrection: Brings us new life in Christ, a life triumphant, our new nature (Romans 5:17; 6:5–11).
- The Ascension: Empowers us with that same authority Jesus Christ has been given—all authority in heaven and on earth (Matthew 28:18; Ephesians 2:4–6).

Here are three different daily prayers I've used over the years to take my place in Christ, in his cross, resurrection and ascension, and gain the victory over the Enemy. The first is simple and straightforward. The second is a bit longer. The third looks long, but after you've been battling a while you'll find it easy to pray 'cause it's really, really powerful. Use what's helpful for you.

Dear Heavenly Father, I honor you as my sovereign Lord. I acknowledge that you are always present with me. You are the only all-powerful and all-wise God. You are kind and loving in all your ways. I love you and I thank you that I am united with Christ and spiritually alive in him. I choose not to love the world, and I crucify my flesh and all its passions. I thank you for the life that I now have in Christ, and I ask you to fill me with your Holy Spirit that I may live my life free from sin. I declare my dependence upon you, and I take my stand against Satan and all his lying ways. I choose to believe the truth, and I refuse to be discouraged. You are the God of all hope, and I am confident that you will meet my needs as I seek to live according to your Word. I express with confidence that I can live a responsible life through Christ who strengthens me. I now take my stand against Satan and command him and all his evil spirits to depart from me. I put on the whole armor of God. I submit my body as a living sacrifice and renew my mind by the living Word of God in order that I may prove that the will of God is good, acceptable, and perfect. I ask these things in the precious name of my Lord and Savior, Jesus Christ. Amen.[2]

SAINT PATRICK'S BREASTPLATE

I arise today
Through a mighty strength, the invocation of the Trinity,
Through belief in the threeness,
Through confession of the oneness
Of the Creator of creation.

I arise today
Through the strength of Christ's birth with his baptism,
Through the strength of his crucifixion with his burial,
Through the strength of his resurrection with his ascension,
Through the strength of his descent for the judgment of Doom.

---

[2] From Neil Anderson's Freedom in Christ Ministries.

I arise today
Through the strength of the love of cherubim,
In obedience of angels,
In the service of archangels,
In hope of resurrection to meet with reward,
In prayers of patriarchs,
In predictions of prophets,
In preaching of apostles,
In faith of confessors,
In innocence of holy virgins,
In deeds of righteous men.

I arise today
Through the strength of heaven:
Light of sun,
Radiance of moon,
Splendor of fire,
Speed of lightning,
Swiftness of wind,
Depth of sea,
Stability of earth,
Firmness of rock.

I arise today
Through God's strength to pilot me:
God's might to uphold me,
God's wisdom to guide me,
God's eye to look before me,
God's ear to hear me,
God's word to speak for me,
God's hand to guard me,
God's way to lie before me,
God's shield to protect me,
God's host to save me

From snares of devils,
From temptations of vices,
From everyone who shall wish me ill,
Afar and anear,
Alone and in multitude.

I summon today all these powers between me and those evils,
Against every cruel, merciless power that may oppose my body and soul,
Against incantations of false prophets,
Against black laws of pagandom,
Against false laws of heretics,
Against craft of idolatry,
Against spells of witches and smiths and wizards,
Against every knowledge that corrupts man's body and soul.

Christ to shield me today
Against poison, against burning,
Against drowning, against wounding,
So that there may come to me abundance of reward.
Christ with me, Christ before me, Christ behind me,
Christ in me, Christ beneath me, Christ above me,
Christ on my right, Christ on my left,
Christ when I lie down, Christ when I sit down, Christ when I arise,
Christ in the heart of every man who thinks of me,
Christ in the mouth of everyone who speaks of me,
Christ in every eye that sees me,
Christ in every ear that hears me.

I arise today
Through a mighty strength, the invocation of the Trinity,
Through belief in the threeness,
Through confession of the oneness,
Of the Creator of creation.[3]

---

[3] From *How the Irish Saved Civilization* by Thomas Cahill.

My dear Lord Jesus, I come to you now to be restored in you—to renew my place in you, my allegiance to you, and to receive from you all the grace and mercy I so desperately need this day. I honor you as my sovereign Lord, and I surrender every aspect of my life totally and completely to you. I give you my body as a living sacrifice, I give you my soul and my spirit as well. I cover myself with your blood—my spirit, my soul, and my body. And I ask your Holy Spirit to restore my union with you, seal me in you, and guide me in this time of prayer. In all that I now pray, I include (my wife and children by name). Acting as their head, I bring them under my authority and covering, and I come under your authority and covering. Holy Spirit, apply to them all that I now pray on their behalf.

Dear God, holy and blessed Trinity, you alone are worthy of all my worship, my heart's devotion, all my praise and all my trust and all the glory of my life. I worship you, bow to you, and give myself over to you in my heart's search for life. You alone are Life, and you have become my life. I renounce all other gods, all idols, and I give you the place in my heart and in my life that you truly deserve. I confess here and now that it is all about you, God, and not about me. You are the Hero of this story, and I belong to you. Forgive me, God, for my every sin. Search me and know me and reveal to me any aspect of my life that is not pleasing to you. And grant me the grace of a deep and true repentance.

Heavenly Father, thank you for loving me and choosing me before you made the world. You are my true Father—my Creator, my Redeemer, my Sustainer, and the true end of all things, including my life. I love you, I trust you, I worship you. Thank you for proving your love for me by sending your only Son, Jesus, to be my substitute and representative. I receive him and all his life and all his work, which you ordained for me. Thank you for including me in Christ, for forgiving my sins, for granting me his righteousness, for making me complete in him. Thank you for making me alive with Christ, raising me with him, seating me with him at your right hand, granting me his authority and anointing me with your Holy Spirit. I receive it all with thanks and give it total claim to my life.

Jesus, thank you for coming for me, for ransoming me with your own life. I honor you as my Lord, I love you, worship you, trust you. I sincerely receive you as my redemption, and I receive all the work and triumph of your crucifixion, whereby I am cleansed from all my sin through your shed blood, my old nature is removed, my heart is circumcised unto God. I take my place in your cross and death, whereby I have died with you to sin, to the flesh, to the world and to the evil one. I am crucified with Christ. I take up my cross and crucify my flesh with all its pride, unbelief, and idolatry. I put off the old man. I bring the cross of Christ between me and all people, all spirits, all things. Holy Spirit, apply to me (my wife and children) the fullness of the work of the crucifixion of Jesus Christ for me. I receive it with thanks and give it total claim to my life.

Jesus, I also sincerely receive you as my new life, my holiness and sanctification, and I receive all the work and triumph of your resurrection, whereby I have been raised with you to a new life, to walk in newness of life, dead to sin and alive to God. I am crucified with Christ and it is no longer I who live but Christ who lives in me. I take my place in your resurrection, putting on the new man in all holiness and humility, in all righteousness and purity and truth. Christ is now my life, the One who strengthens me. Holy Spirit, apply to me (my wife and my children) the fullness of the resurrection of Jesus Christ for me. I receive it with thanks and give it total claim to my life.

Jesus, I sincerely receive you as my everlasting deliverance from and victory over Satan, and I receive all the work and triumph of your ascension, whereby I have been raised with you to the right hand of the Father and established with you in all authority. I take my place in your ascension, whereby I am given fullness in you, in your power, authority, and dominion over every ruler, power, authority, and spiritual force of wickedness. I claim the cross and blood of Jesus Christ against Satan, against his kingdom, and against all his emissaries and all their work against me and my domain. Satan is defeated, the prince of this world is cast down, the rulers and authorities are disarmed. Greater is he who is in me than he who is in the world. Christ has given me authority to overcome all the power of the evil one and I claim that authority now over and against every enemy. Holy Spirit, apply to me (my wife and my children) the fullness of the work of the ascension of Jesus Christ for me. I receive it with thanks and give it total claim to my life.

Holy Spirit, I sincerely receive you as my Counselor, my Comforter, my strength and my guide. Thank you for sealing me in Christ. I ask you to lead me into all truth, to anoint me for all of my life and walk and calling, and to lead me deeper into Jesus today. Apply to me, blessed Holy Spirit, all of the works and all of the gifts in Pentecost. I fully open my life to you in every dimension and aspect, choosing to be filled with you, to walk in step with you in all things. Fill me afresh, blessed Holy Spirit. I receive you with thanks and give you total claim to my life (and my wife and children).

Dear Heavenly Father, thank you for granting to me all spiritual blessings in the heavens in Christ Jesus. I receive those blessings into my life today, and I ask the Holy Spirit to bring all those blessings into my life this day. Thank you for the blood of Jesus. Wash me with his blood from every sin and stain and evil device. Equip me with your armor—the belt of truth, the breastplate of righteousness, the shoes of the gospel, the helmet of salvation. I take up the shield of faith and the sword of the Spirit, the word of God, and I wield these weapons against the evil one in the power of God. I choose to pray at all times in the Spirit.

Heavenly Father, thank you for your angels. I summon them in the authority of Jesus Christ and release them to war for me and my household. Thank you for the intercessors; I ask you to send forth your Spirit and raise them up, arouse them, unite them, establish and direct them, raising up the full canopy of prayer and intercession for me. I call forth the kingdom of the Lord Jesus Christ this day throughout my home, my family, my life.

All this I pray in the name of Jesus Christ, with all glory and honor and thanks to him.[4]

"The kingdom of heaven has been treated violently," said Jesus, "and violent men take it by force" (Matthew 11:12 NASB). Is that a good thing or a bad thing? Do you now see the deep and holy goodness of aggression and strength in men?

If you are going to live in God's kingdom, Jesus says, it's going to take every ounce of passion and forcefulness you've got. Things are going to get fierce; that's why you were given a fierce heart. Do you have something better to do with your life?

Pray the Daily Prayer above!

---

[4] This prayer is adapted from one I found in Ed Murphy's *The Spiritual Warfare Handbook.*

CHAPTER 10

A BEAUTY TO LOVE

Beauty is not only a terrible thing, it is also a mysterious thing.
There God and the Devil strive for mastery,
and the battleground is the heart of men.

DOSTOYEVSKY

BEFORE SETTING OUT

Two things before you start working through this chapter:

First, watch *Titanic* (but turn your eyes for the moment of nudity; it only lasts a few seconds). The film captured the hearts of many, many women and for good reason. As you watch it, ask yourself, *Why? What about a woman's heart did this film speak to so deeply? What is it about Jack that made him so captivating?* Better still, ask your wife what her favorite film is, and watch it, asking yourself as you do, *What is this telling me about my wife's heart? Why does she love* this *movie? What does she want from me that is portrayed here?*

Second, ask your wife to read the chapter, and then carve out an evening where the two of you can talk about it. I'll offer some guidance for that conversation below.

FIELD NOTES

GUT REACTION

As always, start with a gut reaction to the chapter.

GETTING YOUR BEARINGS

The Goal

Most of you will have a woman in your life—your wife, the woman you hope will be your wife, or a woman you are thinking of pursuing. Yes, God does call a few men to singleness—but only a few. For most of us, the Battle for the Beauty is core to our masculine journey. So the goal here is to engage that fight for her more clearly and willfully than we ever have before.

Trail Markers

- Your woman has been asking one question, too, ever since she was young: *Am I lovely?*
- And now the damsel is in distress; she, too, has been wounded in her heart.
- If you ever hope to truly enjoy the Beauty, you are going to have to *fight* for her.
- It's a battle that takes time. The tower comes down one brick at a time.
- You offer your strength for her in order to heal her wound, to help answer her Question with a resounding *YES*.
- But in this battle you cannot take *your* Question to her. Win or lose, this is about the kind of man you want to be.

THE BEAUTY WE LONG FOR

Okay, let's admit it—this is the deepest and hardest battle we ever face. The tower is real, the damsel is in distress, and the dragon isn't just going to roll over and say,

"Sure—take her. Live happily ever after." What is more, this battle cuts to the quick of our own masculinity more than any other. To charge the beaches at Normandy and be taken out by a mortar shell isn't anywhere as personal as going in after your wife and having her shut you down—or laugh in your face. We've all stayed clear of this battle *for a reason*. Am I right? What are you feeling as you think of fighting for your wife's heart, going to a whole new level in your relationship, into waters you've never sailed before?

Bottom line is, you've got to be *compelled*; you've got to be gripped in a deep way if you're going in and staying in on this one. Jesus endured the cross, we're told, "for the joy set before him" (Hebrews 12:2). He faced that gruesome battle and bled his all *because there was something he was after* on the other side, something he wanted and wanted deeply. (That something, by the way, included *you*.)

Think about the rest of your days with the Eve in your life—what do you *want* with her? If you go in, what are you hoping to come out with on the other side? If it could be what you would love it to be, describe it. Pick a scene or two from a movie for each of the following questions. *What do you want with your woman?*

What do you want sexually with her?

What do you want emotionally with her?

What do you want spiritually with her?

EVE'S HEART

It would be good to begin with a refresher on the heart of a woman. Reread pages 16–17 and 36–37 in *Wild at Heart*. What was your woman designed to desire? (She may not act like she desires those things, or anything at all, but stay with the *design* of the feminine heart.)

Can you name a woman you've known who embodies those feminine desires? Do you have a good picture of a truly alive woman? Who is she?

What about your woman—do you see the desires of a woman's heart in her life these days? What has she done with those core desires, with her feminine heart?

Maybe another way of asking that is, what does it feel like to be around your wife, or your woman? Is she *alluring, vulnerable, inviting*? Are those the words that come immediately to mind? Or do you experience her as just *busy*, maybe *controlling*—or perhaps *clingy, demanding*? Choose a handful of words that describe your woman.

If she could become a woman you'd be thrilled to be married to, what would she be? Describe her. What is a truly beautiful woman to you . . .

In the bedroom?

Outside the bedroom?

And what would it be like, what would it do for you if in a year or two your woman looks into your eyes and says, "You have given me something I never thought possible. You've fought for me so amazingly, you've given me such adventure, and I know I am beautiful because of you. Come and enjoy my beauty"? Does the thought of that arouse you, or is it so far from your current reality it simply seems unreachable?

And what does your answer to that question say to you about what you've done with *your* heart, so far as your beauty is concerned? Are you "rarin' to go," hopeful, longing but doubtful, cynical?

10 ——————————————————————————— 0

"rarin' to go"   hopeful   longing but   cynical
                                         doubtful

EVE'S WOUND

Just as every little boy is asking one question, every little girl is, as well. But her question isn't so much about her strength. No, the deep cry of a little girl's heart is *Am I lovely?* Every woman needs to know that she is exquisite and exotic and *chosen*. This is core to her identity, the way she bears the image of God. She wonders, *Will you pursue me? Do you delight in me? Will you fight for me?*

Do you see this core longing in her life today? How? Where? And if not, if she doesn't seem to care at all about being deeply desired and fought for—what does that tell you about what's happened to her heart?

FIELD NOTES

She's been wounded, just like you. Some wounds are obvious, like sexual abuse. Others, like neglect, are harder to see. (She may not even see it at this point.) But because of this broken world, every woman carries a wound at the core of her heart of beauty, and the wound always brings a message with it: *No. You're not beautiful and no one will really fight for you.* Like your wound, hers probably came from her father. Do you know what your wife's wound is, and how it came? Has she ever told you about it? Have you ever asked? If not, do you have a hunch what the message given to her by her father was? How did he speak to her heart's deepest Question?

It would be a gift to help your wife understand her wound, and how it came, and how it's shaped her as a woman. For starters, after she's read the chapter, you might suggest to her the following explorations you did yourself back in chapter 4:

What are some of your favorite memories together with your dad? *Why* are they favorite memories?

Can you recall a time as a little girl when you felt deeply *delighted* in by your father? What happened?

And were moments like that rare, or fairly common?

How intentional was your father in pursuing you? Did he take you on "dates," father-daughter outings? Did he seek to know your heart deeply?

Thinking how every little girl wants to know *Am I lovely?*, what was your father's message to you as a little girl? Why do you say that?

If you did experience delight, or maybe just approval from your father, what was that for? Were they achievements of some kind? Good grades, or good behavior?

WARNING!

In the battle for your woman's heart, you will need to understand her wound and how it came. But this is the scariest place she will ever go with you. You can't just barge in and ask; you must *earn* the right to go there, to be trusted with this. Unless your relationship is deeply committed, open, trusting, and vulnerable, don't start your approach toward her with this question. I'll suggest others at the close of this chapter.

Would you say your father was a violent man, a driven man, a hesitant and passive man, or a dead man?

What is your heart's deepest wound as a woman? Can you put words to it? Do you remember how it was given—the way it came?

And what was the *message* of that wound—or that series of wounds? What did it say to you about yourself as a woman?

Do you have a sense of how that wound is affecting you today? What kind of woman have you become, perhaps as a result of it?

In order to understand your wife's feminine journey, you must also understand her history with men—just as you explored in chapter 5 your history with women. Again, I suggest you first offer these questions below for her own reflection, as a way of helping her name her wound and how it grew. Later, it would be wonderful if she could trust you with this information.

What has been your history with men? List the names of the key men in your life, the men you've had a relationship with or wanted a relationship with. Start with your first love, your first sweetheart, and go right up to the present, including your husband or current relationship. Then, answer the following questions for each man: Who pursued whom? Who initiated the relationship?

What was the relationship like? Was it stormy, placid, passionate, guarded, argumentative, boring?

Who led during the course of the relationship? Who initiated phone calls, chose what you'd do on a date, basically provided the energy behind the relationship? Did that change over time?

How did he make you feel about yourself as a woman? What "grade" did he give you, or make you feel you deserved (or, what grade did you give yourself because of him)?

Who broke up with whom? How was it done . . . and why? Most important, what was the message to you?

Do you find yourself thinking about him still; does he show up in your dreams?

What were you looking for from him? Do you see the way you took your Question to him?

Now, notice the flow of all your relationships—do you see a pattern emerging?

Do you see how it affected you? Is there a message about you as a woman that has taken root?

And what do you feel you're currently getting as a grade from your man? What does that make you want to do?

YOUR PART IN THE WOUND

To battle for your wife, you'll need to know not only what her childhood wound(s) were, but also how you've contributed to them. I confessed that when Stasi married me, she married a frightened, driven man who had an affair with his work because he wouldn't risk engaging a woman he sensed he wasn't enough for. What kind of man did your wife marry when she married you?

Did either of you understand your own wounds at that time?

I realized that I had—like so many men—married for safety. I married a woman I thought would never challenge me as a man. Stasi adored me; what more did I need to do? I wanted to look like the knight, but I didn't want to bleed like one. I was deeply mistaken about the whole arrangement. I didn't know about the tower, or the dragon, nor what my strength was for. Why did you marry your wife? Was it to offer your strength, rescue her heart, sweep her up into a great adventure? Or was it more about safety, or your own search for validation, or sexual satisfaction?

As I said, most romances end up with evenings in front of the TV. Look at the continuum below. Plot three numbers on the line—put a 1 to describe where things started out with your woman, 2 for the midpoint in your years together, and a 3 to mark where you are toward her today.

| Passionate | Comfortable | Volatile anger |
| pursuit | safety | or distant withdrawal |

_____

What have you communicated to her over the years about her deepest Question? Have your words, and more importantly, your actions, told her in a thousand ways, *Yes, you are lovely and worth fighting for?* Give a few examples for why you say yes, or no.

So what would you say your long-term impact has been on her heart over the years? What has living with *you* done to *her*? Have you ever asked yourself that question? If it's hard to answer, what does that say about how aware you've been?

Once you have some understanding of her own life story, her wound and the pattern that developed with men over the years, can you see how you've played right into the Enemy's hand—how you've added to her wound, to the patterns, or at best, how little you've done to heal them intentionally, with understanding?

DISPATCH

When I married my wife my heart was completely gone. I was numb. We got married anyway. She divorced me after ten years of marriage. I know why she left me. I did not know how to love her or fight for her. I was not fighting any battles. I was not taking her on any adventures. She died inside, too . . . but I was a really nice guy. She even told others I was too nice. She was lonely and depressed, and I felt like an empty boy inside.

ERIC

OFFERING YOUR STRENGTH

I used the image of sex as a picture of what a man offers a woman in every area of life. We give ourselves to her, we offer our strength to tear down the walls of the tower and speak to her heart's deepest Question in a thousand ways. Yes, *you are lovely. Yes, there is someone who will fight for you.* We offer our words and actions to express our delight in her.

Let's start with *words.* I know, I know—it's a classic example that a woman uses thousands more words each day than a man, that men don't communicate verbally, and all that. Most of it is excuse making. Your woman craves words from you, longs for conversation with you. Offer it. This is not going to kill you.

How many times a week do you tell your wife that you love her?

How many times a week do you tell your wife that she is lovely, or pretty, that she looks great or that you like what she's wearing?

And in a given week, is it common for the two of you to have a personal conversation about your life or hers, one that lasts more than five minutes?

There's no formula for this, but if you're not speaking to her heart's desire to be delighted in daily, if intimate conversations are less than weekly, you're starving her. Ante up, brother.

WARNING!

I want to offer two very strong words of warning, or maybe, words of *encouragement* as you plan your movement back toward your woman. First, the "tower" that has held your wife's heart—and the defenses she's added herself—it usually comes down one brick at a time. That might seem discouraging at first, but only if you want a quick fix, in which case you're not really talking about playing the man at all. If you are, it's helpful to know it takes time, and all of us falter at first. Don't get discouraged if it feels like two steps forward, one step back. That's how it goes. You don't undo decades of damage in a day.

Second, this cannot be about *your* Question. Remember, ever since the Fall, Eve has been a bottomless pit. You'll offer some wonderful words, and she'll love them . . . and they won't fill her. It will, in some ways, never be "enough." YOU CANNOT TAKE HER RESPONSE AS THE REPORT CARD ON YOU. Keep taking *your* Question to God; ask *him* how you're doing.

Now let's look at your actions:

How often do you offer your wife physical attention without expecting it to lead to sex?

How often do you hold hands, sit on the couch and cuddle as you watch a movie, give her a hug or a kiss with nothing else in mind?

Again, if it's less than daily you've got your mission laid out right there.

   And have you given her flowers, a card, a gift, taken her to dinner or on a getaway trip *for no reason whatsoever?*

These sorts of things should occur several times a year at least.

   I pointed out that Joseph gave up a lot for Mary—business opportunities, church position, even friendships. What sort of sacrifices have you made this year to demonstrate to your wife that she is your priority?

And what is it going to cost you to really fight for her over the next several months?

FROM THE MAP

In his first epistle, Peter gives some crucial advice to wives and husbands. As he does, he uses the same phrase twice, speaking to men and women. He says, "in the same way."

> Wives, in the same way submit yourselves to your own husbands so that, if any of them do not believe the word, they may be won over without words by the behavior of their wives . . .
>
> Husbands, in the same way be considerate as you live with your wives, and treat them with respect as the weaker partner and as heirs with you of the gracious gift of life . . . (1 Peter 3:1, 7)

In *what* "same way"? Look at the passage that precedes this one. He's talking about the crucifixion.

> To this you were called, because Christ suffered for you, leaving you an example, that you should follow in his steps. (2:21)

Peter first points out how Jesus laid it all down for us, did something that looked immensely stupid from a human perspective. He then goes on to say that in order to love each other, we're also going to have to take risks that will feel life-threatening, at least at a soul level. We're going to have to do things that require the kind of faith in God that Jesus had to have when he went to the cross. In other words, if you're not scared, if it doesn't feel really risky, then you're not really moving toward your woman. You're playing it safe.

So, what would feel really threatening to you right now in terms of what you could do to move toward your wife? What would feel really risky? For some of you it will be initiating sex. For others, it will be initiating intimate conversation, or offering to take dance classes with her, or inviting her to a weekend away. What's it going to be for *you*?

THE ENEMY

Don't forget there's a dragon. I told you that my first real moves back toward my wife around our tenth anniversary unleashed a hailstorm of spiritual attack. Heads up. What sort of accusation have you felt around your woman or your marriage in the past? Remember the story I told in chapter 8, about the conversation I heard in my head as I was stuck in the traffic jam? Then there was the one I told you about in this chapter, the trial at the wedding reception. What has the Enemy used against you in the past, when it comes to your woman?

And what are the truths you will use to fight back against him as he comes the next time around?

TALKING ABOUT THIS WITH HER

This chapter—the whole book in fact—can be the turning point in a whole new level of love and redemption in your marriage. But it isn't going to be easy. Certainly you know that by now. You can't expect to undo in a day damage done to her heart over ten, twenty-five, forty years of marriage. You are going to have to fight for her over the long haul. And you're going to have to beware the arrows the Enemy will fire at you with increased anger because you're moving in this direction.

So the thoughts I offer here are a beginning. This is not a formula, and it sure isn't a shortcut to the life you want with her. *The words you use and the approach you take aren't nearly as important as your heart toward her.*

I think you could use this chapter as a launching point for some really good—yes, risky—conversations with her. Start by asking her to read chapter 10 in the book, and express your desire to talk with her about it.

Set aside at least an hour for this first conversation.

I recommend starting with *your* heart toward her. What can you "own up to" by way of your failure to play the man in her life? And, maybe more importantly, what do you want to say to her about the man you *want* to be for her? You might want to refer to some passages from the chapter, explaining that while they may not be your words or even the right words, they do express what you want.

Ask her what struck her in the chapter. Was she moved by anything? Did anything really speak to her heart?

Share with her what the book has meant to you, what God has been doing in your life through this study. Tell her about your wound . . . and then ask her about hers. You might want to offer the exercises I gave above as a way of helping her put some words to her own wound.

Even more vulnerably, ask her how *you've* wounded her over the years. Listen without defending; let her lay it out. Do not rush to get beyond this quickly. Listen carefully, put yourself in her shoes, and own up to it. Accept the way you've damaged her heart. Only then, after you've acknowledged the weight of it, do you ask her to forgive you.

Ask her what she wants with you in the years ahead. Ask her what I asked you—that if life could turn for the better, and your relationship could become what she would love it to be, what would that look like for her? Maybe she, too, could point to a movie as an example. Consider asking her these questions:

What do you want with me emotionally?

What do you want with me spiritually?

What do you want with me physically and sexually?

Now listen, brother—if she is so courageous as to go here with you (maybe not right away, but eventually), and she shares her heart's desire with you, then

WARNING!

Please hear me when I say that none of this is a formula. Your wife is not a problem to be solved; she is a woman to be loved. She doesn't want to be fixed; she wants to be known and delighted in. You can't know what the battle for her heart is about until you know her well and know her story. Spend time with her. Take time every week to talk, and make opportunities for longer time together, too. Make her a priority.

you have been given a priceless treasure few men get. DO IT. Do exactly what she's asked. Oh, not in a day, of course, and not all in a rush to overwhelm her. But if a couple of weeks go by and she sees no change, you do nothing of what she's desired with you, then mister, that tower is going to be so thick when you do get around to it that you'll have missed an incredible opportunity.

ONE FINAL WORD

This isn't going to be easy. Every man I know has taken some painful wounds as he's tried to love the Beauty in his life. The spiritual warfare can get pretty intense, too. And you'll need to fight it as such. As I said, it's not just once, but again and again over time. That's where the myth really stumps us. Some men are willing to go in once, twice, even three times. But a warrior is in this for good. Oswald Chambers asks, "God spilt the life of his Son that the world might be saved; are we prepared to spill out our lives?"

I told you about Daniel, how he's in the midst of a very hard, very unpromising battle for his wife. It's been years now without much progress and without much hope. As we sat together in a restaurant several months ago, tears in his eyes, this is what he said to me: "I'm not going anywhere. This is my place in the battle. This is the hill that I will die on." He has reached a point that we all must come to, sooner or later, when it's no longer about winning or losing. His wife may respond and she may not. That's really no longer the issue. The question is simply this: What kind of man do you want to be? Maximus? Wallace? Or Judah?

Dear God, forgive me for living a selfish, self-protecting life. Forgive me for not spending my life on behalf of my woman, and for all the wounds I've given her. O grant me the grace to undo that damage and bring that tower down. Jesus, awaken me to the real battle for her, expose the Enemy and his tactics against her and against our marriage. Give me your fierce love, your jealous love for my wife and for her freedom. And grant me courage, cunning, and selflessness as I fight for her. I want to be a Wallace for her—not a Judah. I ask this in your name.

CHAPTER 11

AN ADVENTURE TO LIVE

The place that God calls you is the place where
your deep gladness and the world's deep hunger meet.

FREDERICK BUECHNER

BEFORE SETTING OUT

Two things before you start working through this chapter:

First, I recommend watching *The Legend of Bagger Vance*. It is the story of how a man lost heart and his calling, and how an "angel" comes to him to help recover his "authentic swing."

Second, you should take a day off, or better, a weekend—a sabbath completely free of the expectations of anyone and anything in your world. Get away into some wild place—a forest, a field, a lake, or a remote place in the park. Take your journal, and stay with one question all day: "If I could do with my life what I most *want* to do, what would I do?"

GUT REACTION

One last time—start with a gut reaction to the chapter. What are you really struck by? What did this make you want to do?

GETTING YOUR BEARINGS

The Goal

Our goal here is to recover that adventure God wrote on your heart when he made you. Your deepest desires reveal your deepest calling, the adventure God has for you. You must decide whether or not you'll exchange a life of control born out of fear for a life of risk born out of faith. It's high time you get on with that story.

Trail Markers

- Life is not a problem to be solved; it is an adventure to be lived.
- Therefore, a man just won't be happy until he's got adventure in his work, his love, and his spiritual life.
- Yet most men sacrifice their dreams because of fear, and they live out a script someone else wrote for them.
- Your true calling is written on your true heart, and you'll discover it when you enter the frontier of your deep desires.
- Ultimately, this means you forsake a careful life that depends on formulas for an intimate, conversational walk with God.

MADE FOR ADVENTURE

I opened this chapter with the story about Jumping Rock, how wonderful it felt to overcome a fear and discover the thrill of freedom. Have you ever had an experience like that, where you embraced an adventure in spite of your fears, and discovered the thrill of living freely, if only for an afternoon? What was it?

If you have a few extra moments, I want you to recall some of the adventures you've had from the major seasons of your life. When did you *really* experience freedom, exhilaration, take a risk, come alive . . .

As a boy?

As a teen/young man?

As a grown man?

After telling of how we "hurled ourselves" out into the middle of the canyon, and free-falling for what felt like enough time to say the Gettysburg Address and then plunging into the river, I said, "I want to live my whole life like that." What was your reaction?

ASKING THE RIGHT QUESTION

I told the story of how I became an author and a counselor, how that journey began with these simple words:

Don't ask yourself what the world needs. Ask yourself what makes you come alive, and go do that, because what the world needs is people who have come alive.

Is that the question you asked yourself that led to the life *you* are living now? If not, what was the question you asked that resulted in the life you now have?

found myself at a sort of crossroads: Down one road was my dream and desire, which I had no means to pay for and an absolutely uncertain future after that; down the other was a comfortable step up the ladder of success, a very obvious next career move and the total loss of my soul. Have you ever stood at a crossroads like that—where one path was a dream you could follow and the other was a

FIELD NOTES

practical path that offered safety and predictability? What did you do? Is that what your heart most wanted to do?

The diagram below divides men into four groups based on how much they embrace God and risk. Men in Quadrant 1 may be spiritual, but it's a safe or controlling spirituality. These are hesitant men who justify their cautiousness by calling it spiritual. Or, they might be controlling men, who practice their religion as tips and techniques that allow them to control their world. (I might note that if a man moves up the vertical axis toward a true intimacy with God, he won't stay in Quadrant 1 for long. God will hurl him into Quadrant 4.) The men in Quadrant 2 are also men who live "safely," but they have no spiritual disguise for it. They hide behind the newspaper or their work. Men in Quadrant 3 may be entrepreneurs or they may be gamblers or extreme sports addicts. They are men with a great deal of so-called adventure in their lives, but it is a totally godless adventure. Men in Quadrant 4 are guys like King David or the apostle Paul or Christopher Columbus—men who venture forth on a quest of great risk because they are walking with God.

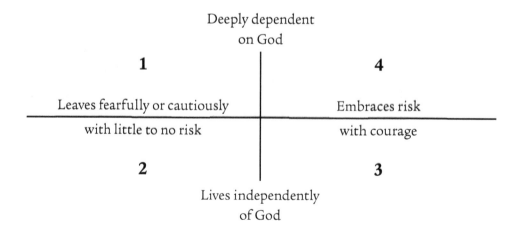

Where would you place yourself? Why?

Too many men forsake their dreams because they aren't willing to risk, or fear they aren't up to the challenge, or are never told that those desires deep in their heart are *good*. If you left some or even all your dreams by the side of the road, which of these three reasons was the reason why? Can you remember what motivated you to forsake your dreams—what might be blocking you from pursuing them still?

WHAT ARE YOU WAITING FOR?

Let's go back to why God made man in the first place—why he made *you*. In chapter 3 I said,

> Why does God create Adam? What is a man for? If you know what something is designed to do, then you know its purpose in life. A retriever loves the water; a lion loves the hunt; a hawk loves to soar. It's what they're made for. Desire reveals design, and design reveals destiny. In the case of human beings, our design is also revealed by our desires. Let's take adventure. Adam and all his sons after him are given an incredible mission: rule and subdue, be fruitful and multiply. "Here is the entire earth, Adam. Explore it, cultivate it, care for it—it is your kingdom." Whoa . . . talk about an invitation. This is permission to do a heck of a lot more than cross the street. It's a charter to find the equator; it's a commission to build Camelot. Only Eden is a garden at that point; everything else is wild, so far as we know. No river has been charted, no ocean crossed, no mountain climbed. No one's discovered the molecule, or fuel injection, or Beethoven's *Fifth*. It's a blank page, waiting to be written. A clean canvas, waiting to be painted.
>
> Most men think they are simply here on earth to kill time—and it's killing them. But the truth is precisely the opposite. The secret longing of

your heart, whether it's to build a boat and sail it, to write a symphony and play it, to plant a field and care for it—those are the things you were made to do. That's what you're here for. Explore, build, conquer—you don't have to tell a boy to do those things for the simple reason that it *is his purpose.*

Genesis makes it clear why we long for adventure, to hurl ourselves into a creative work worthy of God. It's why he made us.

FROM THE MAP

Now when David had served God's purpose in his own generation, he fell asleep . . . (Acts 13:36)

God raised David up to be king over Israel, and to deliver them from their enemies. That was his destiny. Now listen to how David described it:

The king rejoices in your strength, Lord.
How great is his joy in the victories you give!
You have granted him his heart's desire . . . (Psalm 21:1–2)

What God *called* David to do was exactly what David *wanted* to do. There are so many other examples. Paul was called to be an apostle, and that's what he loved to do. No matter what town or situation he found himself in, he started doing apostle-like things. His calling was his desire. Nehemiah was called by God to rebuild the walls of Jerusalem . . . and that's what his heart *ached* to do. On and on it goes.

Take delight in the Lord
and he will give you the desires of your heart. (Psalm 37:4)

Obviously, God is not the enemy of desire. Furthermore, he "gives" us our desires in two ways. He puts them in our heart, and then he fulfills them.

So, if you had permission to do what you really want to do, what would you do? Don't ask yourself right now what the world needs, ask yourself what makes you come alive. Just start making a list of all the things you deeply desire to do with your life, great and small. And remember—*Don't ask yourself, "How?" How* is never the right question; *how* is a faithless question. *How* is God's department. He is asking you *What*. What is written on your heart? What makes you come alive? If you could do what you've always wanted to do, what would it be?

Often it takes time for a man to recover his heart's desire. I suggest you get away from the noise and distraction of your daily life for time with your own soul. Head into the wilderness, to silence and solitude. Alone with yourself, allow whatever is there to come to the surface. You might want to spend some alone time adding to your list above, and going through some of the exercises I suggest below. After all, this is your *life* we're talking about. You can give it a day or a weekend of reflection.

Once you've made a list of the things you'd love to do with your life, look it over—do you see any *themes* emerging? Could you place an urgency on some desires over others? *This I'd love to do, but this I'll die if I never do.*

Sometimes our dreams are buried deep and it takes some unearthing to get to them. Often the clues are in our past, in those moments when we found ourselves loving what we were doing. The details and circumstances change as we grow, but the themes remain the same. Do a simple survey of your life, thinking back over those moments when you really loved what you were doing.

What did you most enjoy in school? What were your favorite subjects? Best moments?

When you walk into a bookstore, what section do you go to?

How about jobs you really loved, or better, assignments within a job that you truly enjoyed?

A BREAK IN THE CLOUDS

Not all desires are the same. Not all adventures have the same weight to them. Borrowing from some categories Larry Crabb used in *Inside Out*, I want to try to bring some clarity to this whole idea of adventure.

Casual Adventures include the things you'd love to do with a vacation, or a free weekend, or some spare time. The risk involved is minimal to mild—some wasted time, a loss of discretionary income, physical injury perhaps. This sort of adventure stretches you beyond your comfort zone, and that's a healthy thing to do.

Critical Adventures involve the major arenas of your life—your relationships, your work, your church community. The risk here feels huge, sometimes even life-threatening at a soul level. Drawing a line in the sand on an issue at work or in the church, entering into a deep friendship, or moving toward your wife can feel risky indeed. This sort of adventure stretches you to the limit of your personal resources, well beyond what you thought you were able to do. As you stand on the precipice you wonder, *Have I got what it takes?*

Crucial Adventures also involve the major arenas of your life, only there is one crucial difference—God *has* to show up if it's going to work out. These most import-ant of all adventures are a direct result of our following God into the unknown, as Peter followed Christ onto the sea, or as Abraham left all he had to go with God into the destiny of his life. You know you can't succeed in this sort of adventure without the supernatural intervention of God. As you stand on the precipice you wonder, *Has God got what it takes (will he come through)?*

Were there some times in your life when people said, "Wow—you really impacted me"? What were you doing?

Using the idea that Jesus is our Prophet, Priest, and King, I find that men tend to fall into one of thwose categories when it comes to their desires and their calling. *Kings* love to build, invest, create, and care for the realm. They are concerned about order and prosperity and a good life for those under their care. They tend to be in leadership roles—the presidents of colleges or the heads of corporations or small businesses they start themselves. *Priests* love to care for people on a more personal basis. Obviously, they care for the soul and may actually be priests, or they spend all their volunteer time teaching Bible study. But they may also be doctors or counselors or in some "helping" profession. *Prophets* love to shake the system, to bring people back to the truth. They see beneath the surface of things and have to speak what they see. Some counselors are more prophetic; other prophets might be journalists or teachers or authors (yep).

Now look over your desires list and your life survey. Do you see a Prophet, Priest, or King theme emerging?

Sometimes when we get away and allow our soul a chance to come up for air, what we first encounter is *grief* for so much lost time. There, beneath the grief, are desires long forsaken. What are your deepest regrets about your life? What are the desires you abandoned, the dreams you *didn't* follow?

INTO THE UNKNOWN

Okay, hopefully some of your true heart and true desires are beginning to surface—they may have been surfacing since chapter 1 (that is my hope!). As you stand again at the crossroads, or what may feel like the *precipice*, you are going to face two obstacles to embracing the Adventure—especially the Critical and Crucial Adventures. Those obstacles are fear and mystery (or simply the unknown).

Howard Macey said, "The spiritual life cannot be made suburban; it is always frontier and we who live in it must accept and even rejoice that it remains untamed." Mystery is essential to adventure. Mystery is the heart of the universe and the God who made it. The most important aspects of your world—your relationship with God and with the people in your life, your calling, the spiritual

WARNING!

Obviously, I am not suggesting that every desire we have is good, nor that every desire reflects God's will for us. Romans 8 says that the desires of our flesh war against the desires of the Spirit of God in us, the new man, the new heart. I said, "The invitation in the book shop, I must note, was given to me some years into my Christian life when the transformation of my character was at a point I could hear it without running off and doing something stupid. I've met men who've used advice like it as permission to leave their wife and run off with their secretary. They are *deceived* about what it is they really want, what they are made for." As Paul said, "So I say, walk by the Spirit, and you will not gratify the desires of the flesh" (Galatians 5:16).

battles you'll face—every one of them is fraught with mystery. Does that seem like a bad thing to you, as you stand on the precipice?

The poet David Whyte says, "The price of our vitality is the sum of all our fears." What are the major fears you have as you embark on the adventures God is stirring in you?

And what will you do with those fears and with the unknown? We have three choices—(1) to shrink back, as so many of us have done before, and reject the invitation to Adventure; (2) to try to reach for some sort of formula that will give us a sense of control; or (3) to simply venture forward with God. This is the moment our true strength begins to be released. As I said, "[This] is where our strength will be crystallized, deepened and *revealed*. A man is never more a man than when he embraces an adventure beyond his control, or when he walks into a battle he isn't sure of winning." What are you feeling tempted to do? Can you distinguish the voices of your false self, your Enemy, and your true heart?

"Perfect love drives out fear," says the apostle John (1 John 4:18). There may be direct biblical promises that address your fears, promises about financial provision (Matthew 6:25–34; Philippians 4:19; Hebrews 13:5–6), promises for spiritual protection (John 10:1–18; 1 John 5:18). But ultimately, we must take our fears to God, who is perfect love, and ask him to speak to them personally. One thing we know—God will never remove the element of faith from our lives. Walking with him will always involve risk. That is why following God into the Adventures he has for us always comes down to, *Will you trust me?* For what he offers us is *himself.*

FROM FORMULA TO RELATIONSHIP

The problem with modern Christianity's obsession with principles is that it removes any real conversation with God. Find the principle, apply the principle—what do you need God for? Would you say your Christian life has been more oriented toward rules and regulations, or a personal relationship with God?

There are no formulas with God. Period. So there are no formulas for the man who follows him. God is a person, not a doctrine. He operates not like a system—not even a theological system—but with all the originality of a truly free and alive person. "The realm of God is dangerous," says Archbishop Anthony Bloom. "You must enter into it and not just seek information about it."

The only way to live in this adventure—with all its danger and unpredictability and immensely high stakes—is in an ongoing, intimate relationship with God. I used Moses and Abraham and David as examples, but the danger in doing that is some men will say, "Well sure, that was true for Moses and Abraham and David, but c'mon now—I'm just an ordinary guy, not a patriarch out of the Bible." Do you think that sort of conversational intimacy, where God speaks to you personally, is available to you? If not, why not? What is your position based on—Scripture, or experience?

A BREAK IN THE CLOUDS

Let me make something clear: God does give us principles that are true about every human life. The book of Proverbs is full of them: "Lazy hands make for poverty . . . stay away from a foolish man . . . a gentle answer turns away wrath" (10:4; 14:7; 15:1). I am not dismissing the wisdom of these principles. What I am saying is that (1) principles are never enough, and (2) neither are they the goal of the Christian life. They are never enough because you will encounter unique situations that seem to defy wisdom. "Don't get out of a boat in the middle of a lake in the middle of the night and try to walk home" would be a good principle, generally speaking. But Jesus tells Peter to get out of the boat and walk on the water. Furthermore, principles are not the goal of the Christian life—*intimacy with God* is. A man who stays in a Christianity of tips and techniques will eventually find himself confused, overwhelmed, bored, and distant from God.

I spoke to the issue of hearing from God in chapter 7 of this field guide, when I talked about hearing our new name. It might be helpful to revisit those ideas. And let me offer a few more words of guidance here:

Learning to hear the voice of God in our hearts and recognize his hand in our lives is something that is *cultivated* over time. We grow into it; we learn to discern between our thoughts and his voice and the voice of the Enemy (who loves to play the ventriloquist, by the way, and make you think it's the voice of God). Don't be frustrated if you do not hear, or it seems cloudy, or you go through periods of "silence." We don't become *intimate* allies with God overnight, but over a lifetime.

I always hear better when my heart has been tuned to Christ through worship, or devotional reading, or through silence and solitude. It's very hard to rush in from the chaos of a day and seek guidance in twenty seconds. And it's a given that I cannot hear when I am "in the flesh," when I am not walking by God's Spirit. Tune your heart in first. Then ask your questions.

Lay your agenda on the altar. I find it very hard to hear from God when I refuse to hear any answer but the one I want to hear. In order to hear a "yes" with confidence, I have to be willing to hear a "no."

If you are uncertain whether it is God who is "speaking," then do what John says; "test the spirits" (1 John 4:1). When God speaks in our hearts, the message will never contradict Scripture. The written Word of God is always our benchmark; all other words are tested against it. Also, is it consistent with other things God has made clear to you over the years? Does it ring true with your new heart, with the Spirit of God within you? Finally, what is the effect of what you're hearing—does it rouse hope and require faith? God's voice does not discourage or condemn or elicit fear (Romans 8:1; 2 Timothy 1:7).

Last, when it comes to critical and crucial questions, ask God for a confirmation of what you have heard—a Scripture that affirms it, or a word of counsel from a godly ally, or an event that sheds further light on the matter.

It might be helpful to keep in mind that we are in a journey, and the nature of that journey is God initiating us into our full strength, our new name, our place in his kingdom. Our whole journey into authentic masculinity centers around those cool-of-the-day talks with God. Simple questions change hassles to adventures; the events of our lives become opportunities for initiation. "What are you teaching me here, God? What are you asking me to do . . . or to let go of? What in my heart are you speaking to?" Do you sense what God is saying to you about those questions even now? Why not ask him? Take an event that's unfolding right now in your life, and bring those questions to him about it.

FIELD NOTES

A BREAK IN THE CLOUDS

There is a beautiful balance given to us in the book of Acts, when the apostles are needing to choose good men to help them with their ministry.

> Brothers . . . choose seven men from among you who are known to be full of the Spirit and wisdom. (Acts 6:3)

In this dangerous life God has called us to, we are going to need both wisdom and revelation—sound guidance and direct words from God—if we hope to make it through.

FURTHER UP AND FURTHER IN

There comes the baffling call of God in our lives also. The call of God can never be stated explicitly; it is implicit. The call of God is like the call of the sea, no one hears it but the one who has the nature of the sea in him. It cannot be stated definitely what the call of God is to, *because his call is to be in comradeship with himself* for his own purposes, and the test is to believe that God knows what He is after. (Oswald Chambers, italics mine)

My guess is, the journey that now lies ahead of you doesn't seem real clear. Am I right? That's not a bad sign—that doesn't mean you're not "getting it." Not at all. The call of God always, *in every case*, requires deeper intimacy with God. I don't know one man to whom God has given the entire game plan for his life. Not one. You want to know something fascinating? Not even Jesus has the full game plan! (See *From the Map* on page 278.)

All God usually reveals to us is a big vision, written in our desire, and the next couple of steps. Consider that an act of mercy. If he had told you all that was going to happen in your life up to *this* point, would you have really wanted to know?

So let's take it a step at a time. Casual Adventures are not unspiritual because they are casual. For many of us, they are a starting point, where we learn to sort of flex our soul's muscles, if you will. They should lead us and prepare us for Critical Adventures, which we're going to have to embrace or we'll remain selfish, self-centered men. Critical Adventures build us up to Crucial Adventures, the deep destiny of our lives.

All the while we are asking, "What is the desire *beneath* this desire?" What is it I am really yearning for?" As I said, we all have desires in our hearts that are core

FROM THE MAP

They [will] see the Son of Man coming on the clouds of heaven, with power and great glory. And he will send his angels with a loud trumpet call, and they will gather his elect from the four winds, from one end of the heavens to the other . . . About that day or hour no one knows, not even the angels in heaven, *nor the Son*, but only the Father.

MATTHEW 24:30–31, 36
emphasis added

to who and what we are; but they are *mythic* in their meaning, waking in us something transcendent and eternal. We can be mistaken about how those desires will finally be fulfilled, and that's okay. *How* isn't our department, remember?

Ours is simply to enter in, follow what we have in front of us, and *let the clarity unfold in the journey.*

Move on to chapter 12, and write the next chapter of your life.

Yes, Lord!
Give me a spirit that on this life's rough sea
Loves to have his sails fill'd with a lusty wind
Even till his sail-yards tremble, his masts crack,
And his rapt ship runs on her side so low
That she drinks water, and her keel ploughs air!

I want to love with much more abandon and stop waiting for others to love me first. I want to hurl myself into a creative work worthy of you, God. I want to charge the fields at Bannockburn, follow Peter as he followed you out onto the sea. Give me your great heart within me to live the adventure you have for me. In Jesus' name.

CHAPTER 12

WRITING THE NEXT CHAPTER

> Freedom is useless if we don't exercise it as characters making choices . . . We are free to change the stories by which we live. Because we are genuine characters, and not mere puppets, we can choose our defining stories. We can do so because we actively participate in the creation of our stories. We are co-authors as well as characters. Few things are as encouraging as the realization that things can be different and that we have a role in making them so.
>
> **DANIEL TAYLOR**

Now, reader, it is your turn to write—venture forth with God.

A BATTLE TO FIGHT

What great battle would you love to devote your life to? What do you want to be different about the world or about the church or about someone's life because you lived?

And what is the next step, the next move you need to make in order to move toward that vision?

Will you do it? When?

AN ADVENTURE TO LIVE

What great adventure would you love to enter into? (No doubt all three of these Core Desires are going to be related somehow.) What quest would you love to take?

And what is the next step, the next move you need to make in order to move toward that vision?

Will you do it? When?

A BEAUTY TO LOVE

Who is the woman God has called you to fight for? (Of course, some of you won't have an answer for this right now. That's okay. This can apply to women in your family, female friends, or the woman who may one day come.) What is the impact you want your life to have upon hers?

And, what is the next step you need to take in order to move toward her, fight for her?

Will you do it? When?

O God, dear Jesus . . . thank you for the work you have done in my life thus far. Lord, all I can say is . . . I want more! More courage, more conviction, more healing, more vision, more of you. Carry me on in this great Quest. When I falter, quicken me. When I fail, encourage me again. And as I move into my true strength and my true place in your great story, O God, all the praise and glory will be to you. I am in this for good. In Jesus' name.

DISPATCH

I am ready.

Not physically, not financially, not socially, not academically, not practically, not politically, not occupationally. Not when ANYTHING visible is considered am I a fit specimen for a wild adventure. And at times I'm not even sure of myself spiritually. "With many a conflict, many a doubt . . . fighting fears within, without . . ."

But thanks be to God, my heart is "in the trim." And he whose name is faithful and true can work with me just as I am. I am certain of him.

CURTIS

Let me close with the passage I began with in the Introduction. You've come far enough now that this is about *you*, valiant one:

> It is not the critic who counts; not the man who points out how the strong man stumbles, or where the doer of deeds could have done them better. The credit belongs to the man in the arena, whose face is marred by dust and sweat and blood; who strives valiantly . . . who knows the great enthusiasms, the great devotions; who spends himself in a worthy cause; who at the best knows in the end the triumph of high achievement, and who at the worst, if he fails, at least fails while daring greatly, so that his place shall never be with those cold and timid souls who have never known neither victory nor defeat.
>
> Teddy Roosevelt

FIELD NOTES

ABOUT THE AUTHOR

John Eldredge is a bestselling author, a counselor, and a teacher. He is also president of Wild at Heart, a ministry devoted to helping people discover the heart of God, recover their own hearts in God's love, and learn to live in God's kingdom. John and his wife, Stasi, leave near Colorado Springs, Colorado.

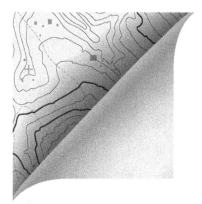

Finishing this Field Guide is only the beginning.

Continue your journey at
WildAtHeart.org

Weekly Podcasts

Video & Audio Resources

Prayers We Pray

Live Events

 Download the **Wild at Heart App**.

Download on the **App Store**   GET IT ON **Google Play**